# From Vacillation to Resolve

# From Vacillation to Resolve

*The French Communist Party in the Resistance, 1939–1944*

Julian Lenwood McPhillips Jr.

NewSouth Books

Montgomery

NewSouth Books
105 S. Court Street
Montgomery, AL 36104

Cataloging-in-Publication Data
ISBN 978-1-58838-379-2 (trade cloth)
ISBN 978-1-58838-381-5 (trade paper)
ISBN 978-1-58838-380-8 (ebook)

A senior thesis submitted to the
History Department of Princeton University
in partial fulfillment of the requirements for
the degree of Bachelor of Arts,
April 17, 1968

and republished in book form
exactly 50 years later,
April 17, 2018

APRIL 1968

*This thesis is dedicated with love to my parents,*
*to whom I am indebted in so many ways.*

APRIL 2018

*This republication fifty years later is dedicated with*
*love to my wife Leslie, children Rachel, Grace, and*
*David, and grandchildren Laurel, Jude, Nanette,*
*Sage, and Emma.*

*Finally, this effort having transformed from a senior*
*thesis into a book, is also dedicated to the memories*
*and great honor of the many brave Resistance fighters*
*who sacrificed all, namely their lives, in ultimately*
*defeating the Nazi menace that threatened their*
*country and the world, 1938–1944.*

# Contents

# Acknowledgments

I would like to express my appreciation first of all to M. and Mme. Roger Pansart of Paramé, near St. Malo, France. They initially stimulated my interest in the general subject of the French Resistance in the summer of 1965, only 20 years after the end of World War II. Driving me around the *départment* of *Ille et Vilaine* in their car, they showed me a number of places where different Resistance actions had taken place. At the same time they told me many stories about their own actions and gave me several interesting comments on the Communists.

At one location in Bretagne, the northwestern province of France, Ms. Pansart showed me where her brother was one of thirteen Resistance fighters captured by the Nazis. All were scheduled to be executed immediately, but the Nazi captain had a list of only twelve names and didn't want to execute one too many. By random selection, her brother was temporarily spared, and afterwards managed to escape. Such hair-raising stories caused my interest to soar.

The Pansarts also proudly showed me medals they had won from Churchill, Roosevelt, and de Gaulle. They were so proud, and I was awed.

Appreciation is also due to Henri Michel, the premier French historian of the Second World War, he gave me much valuable background information. This was during the summer of 1967 when I returned to France, armed with a grant from Princeton's Woodrow Wilson School to do my research. Michel was also helpful in directing me to certain primary sources and the proper libraries in Paris. This included surviving members of the Maquis, the leading French Resistance fighters, who were still alive during the mid-1960s. I was thrilled to meet them.

Great appreciation is due Lill Neace for the re-typing of the original thesis, to enable it to pass electronically into a book form fifty years later. Enormous appreciation is also due Randall Williams and Suzanne La Rosa for their publishing of this book through NewSouth Books, Montgomery, Alabama.

# FROM VACILLATION TO RESOLVE

# Introduction

The role of the Communist party in the French Resistance movement against the Nazis in the Second World War has been the subject of much controversy and dispute but of little research. The lack of research is largely due to the dearth of primary source materials, whereas the controversy centers around the early vacillation of the Communist party and its later allegedly covert challenges to de Gaulle's leadership within the organization in order to obtain a prominent post-war position, if not eventual take-over.

Henri Michel, the premier historian on the subject of the French Resistance, has said that:

> . . . Of all the forces of the clandestine (French) Resistance, the Communist party is the most singular and the most difficult to study. . . . No one else offers as many difficulties for disentangling the true from the false, the apparent from reality. It is to this purpose that judgments the most contradictory have been and are still set forth. In all conscience, an objective study must contain a good share of hypotheses.[1]

Perhaps these limitations to which Michel refers are additional reason for the lack of research on the French Communist role. A. Rossi has made an extensive study of the period from mid-1939

---

1    Henri Michel, *Les Courants de Pensée de la Résistance* (Paris, 1962), p. 555.

to the end of 1941.[2] Alfred Rieber has dealt with the relationship between the Soviet and French Communist actions during the war.[3] Other historians have superficially discussed the actions of the French Communists during the war in general histories of European Communism or the French Communist party.[4] However, to my knowledge, no one has attempted to trace specifically the French Communist role in their opposition to the Nazis from the outbreak of World War II up to the liberation of France. This study is such an attempt.

Admitting the difficulties for interpretation, which Michel mentions, and taking cognizance of the dearth of available primary sources, this presentation will neither attempt to disentangle nor reconcile contradictory judgments, nor presume to be comprehensive. Instead, it will attempt to present an accurate and concise account of just what the French Communists were doing to combat the Germans from August 1939 to August 1944.

Before plunging into greater detail, a brief review of some of the major points to be considered will give the reader a better initial framework for understanding what will be presented later.

The behavior of the French Communists during the Resistance can be divided into three stages, each one marked by a different

2    A. Rossi (Angelo Tasca), *Les Communistes Francais Pendant la Drôle de Guerre* (Paris, 1951), deals with period of "Phony War" and Fall of France, August 1939-July 1940; Physiologie du Parti Communiste Francais (Paris, 1948), deals with structure and organization of the party up to June 1941; *La Guerre des Papillons* (Paris, 1954), treats the use of propaganda, especially tracts, for political purposes during the war, but concentrates mainly on 1941. All three of these books have invaluable reproductions of a variety of primary source materials, including newspapers, pamphlets, letters, and tracts, which together make a major contribution towards understanding the first two stages of the P.C.F. effort.

3    Alfred Rieber, *Stalin and the French Communist Party* (New York, 1962).

4    Jacques Fauret, *L'Histoire du Parti Communiste Français* (Paris, 1948); Gérald Walters, *L'Histoire du Parti Communiste Français* (Paris, 1948); Franz Borkenau, *European Communism* (London, 1953).

policy as will as a progressively longer period of time. The first stage was a very short one, lasting only from August to September 1939. This period involved an almost automatic anti-fascist reflex which animated the activity of the Communists but was disconcerted by repression. Even after the Russo-German Pact, the French Communists were hesitant to change positions until their leaders had been alerted by Moscow.

The second stage lasted from October 1939 to June 22, 1941. The leadership of the French Communist party (P.C.F.) abandoned the preceding position following a severe criticism of the Communist International by the French government and precise orders from Moscow to change positions. A Soviet pamphlet containing an article by Dimitrov, which stated that it was the worker's duty to wage a fearless fight against the imperialist war, also helped to cause this "change of heart." Denouncing the war in its most uncomplimentary terms, as "capitalist" and "imperialist," the Party fought vigorously against the war governments of Daladier and Reynaud. Through its very effective propaganda work and by sabotage of the production of war materials, the Communists did much to hamper the French war effort.

Following the fall of France, the Communists advocated fraternizing with the German soldiers. They asked the Germans for the legal protection of the Communist press and proposed that the government of Vichy be replaced. In one word, the leadership of the P.C.F. wanted, in its relationship with the Occupier, to adopt the "modus vivendi" which had been adopted by the Germans and Soviets in signing their pact. Although the Nazis did not reciprocate, they tolerated the Communists and allowed them a brief "semi-legality." In the last few months before the German attack on Russia, relations between the Occupier and the P.C.F. deteriorated.

However, it should be noted that, during this period, there were some Communists, a fairly numerous group, who left the party in order to resist actively the Germans on their own initiative and outside of the directives set by their leadership.[5]

The third stage lasted from June 22, 1941, to the Liberation in August of 1944. This stage was not subject to dispute by individual members of the Communist party. There was little room for confusion or mixed loyalties after Hitler attacked the Soviet Union. Fighting both for the Soviet Union, the worker's homeland, and for France, the native land, all members of the P.C.F. entered into the Resistance with courage and self-denial. From sabotage work to continuing distribution of the Communist clandestine press to organized guerrilla (maquis) fighting, the Communists were among the most active and most effective members of the Resistance effort. Their long experience as an underground organization gave the Communists a discipline, a unity, and a coordination that were missing in other Resistance organizations, and consequently they obtained a much higher degree of effectiveness in their efforts.

With a broadened base, which included a number of front organizations, the Communists attracted many non-Communist followers, who served their purposes. At the same time, the P.C.F. was very successful at infiltrating other Resistance organizations. Though sporting the Gaullist icon and paying nominal allegiance to his leadership, the Communists were covertly organizing their plans and making preparations for an eventual power base in the post-war government. Conflict between the Communists and Gaullists existed not only on the level of post-war plans but also on the question of tactics to use in the Resistance.

By the German attack against the U.S.S.R. the war had changed in character for the French Communists. From an imperialistic war it became for them a war for the defense of liberty.

---

5 Auguste Lecoeur, a letter to the author, January 18, 1968, p. 2.

# Part One

# Vacillation

AUGUST 23, 1939–JUNE 22, 1941

# Chapter I

# First Stage

**BACKGROUND**

The rise of Adolph Hitler and his National Socialist (Nazi) party in Germany brought an immediate and instinctively negative reaction from the International Communist movement. The French Communists were no exception. Her sister Communist party in Germany had been one of the staunchest opponents of the Nazis, who gained their strongest supporters from the bourgeoisie, the professionals, and the conservative businessmen. Accordingly, one of Hitler's first acts in establishing his totalitarian Third Reich and consolidating his power was to outlaw the German Communist party, the defender of labor interests and the working-class man.

In reciprocation, the Communists were among the earliest in France to voice their opposition to the Nazi regime. Spurred by Communist leadership, "the French working-class (was) the only class," according to Werth, up until the Russo-German pact of August 23, 1939, "which had been powerfully, violently anti-Hitler."[6] In the September 7, 1938, issue of *L'Humanité*, the central organ of the party, the French Communists defined the limits of their hate for the Germans. They said:

> The French people do not confuse and will not confuse the German people with the executioners who, unable to give

---

6    Alexander Werth, *The Twilight of France* (New York, 1942), p. 346.

bread to the workers and to the peasants, want to kill them on the battle fields.

The France of the Popular Front does not confuse the Germany of Beethoven, of Goethe, of Kant, and of Schiller, which it admires and loves, with the Germany of the concentration camps of Hitlerism.

German people, who want peace and who want the grandeur of your country by work and not by war, you must know that, if Hitler unleashes his war, he will find facing him material and moral forces the depth of which he does not suspect.[7]

The French Communists continued to display their active dislike of Hitler and his capitalist war-mongers. The party demanded unyielding opposition to the foreign policy of the Reich and damned as traitors all who had sought to direct attention to the actual power relations between France and Germany. It insisted upon an immediate and unconditional alliance with the U.S.S.R. It fought against the agreements and "spirit" of Munich. It sang the praises of Poland for its "resistant" attitude in the Danzig crisis—and those of England and France for the guarantees that made such an attitude possible.[8] Many French Communists proclaimed that they were willing to "mourir pour Dantzig,"[9] that is, they were willing to make the ultimate sacrifice to help the Polish defeat the Hitlerite imperialists.

The Communists urged all "Frenchmen who want to live free and in peace to be united in order to show Hitler and his agents that we want to remain masters of our own destinies and that we

7   René *Lefeuvre, La Politique Communiste (Paris, 1946), p. 13.*

8   A. Rossi, *Physiologie du Parti Communiste Français* (Paris, 1948), p. 2. Hereafter abbreviated *P.P.C.F.*

9   A. Rossi, *Les Communistes Français Pendant la Drôle de Guerre* (Paris, 1951). Hereafter abbreviated *L.C.F.*

are enemies of international fascism."[10] At this time the Communists were united, though insecurely so, with the Socialists and the Radicals in the Popular Front, with Edouard Daladier as head of the Ministry. France, however, was a worried and disorganized country in the process of preparing itself materially and psychologically for war. The French people were tired of constant partial mobilizations, Hitler's arrogance, and economic uncertainty.[11] Although the Communists had never been a largely respected political party, they were still a legal and important element in French political life.

## NAZI-SOVIET PACT

The signing of the Nazi-Soviet Pact brought about a complete reassessment of the French Communist party by its membership and by non-Communist Frenchmen. At first the party leadership was hesitant, and this period of wavering in August and September of 1939, a very awkward time for French Communists, can be described as the first stage of the role of the party in their resistance effort against the Nazis in World War II.

For several weeks following August 23, 1939, the Communist leaders remained in a state of troubled uncertainty. Not having been notified in advance, French Communists were jolted by the signing of the Pact. As loyal Communists, they were well aware of their allegiance to the worker's homeland, the U.S.S.R., and to their responsibility to heed the directives of the Comintern. Yet the leaders of the P.C.F. were somewhat imprisoned in the anti-Nazi positions which they had held for four years. Thus it was difficult for them to respond quickly to the changing circumstances. Since direct orders had not yet arrived from Moscow, the confused party leaders stated again on August 26, 1939 that it was still necessary to defend Poland:

10    Lefeuvre, p. 14.
11    Werth, p. 345.

> The task of the present is to unite all Frenchmen, to unite
> them against Hitler, the most beastial representative of Fascism,
> toward whom the Communist party is more than ever the
> implacable enemy.[12]

Thus, on the 1st of September they joined in with other non-party members of the Parliament in voting the credits for national defense. Maurice Thorez, the president of the Communist parliamentary group and the Secretary-General of the P.C.F., affirmed at that time "the unshaken resolve of all Communists to take their places in the front lines of resistance against the aggression of Hitlerian Fascism."[13]

And, then, on September 6, 1939, Marcel Cachin, known by many in the party as the "venerate leader," wrote:

> After the aggression against Poland the French Communist
> party maintains toward Hitlerism the attitude it always held. It
> declares that a primary duty is imposed on all workers: it is to
> accept the measures of military order demanded by the govern-
> ment to defeat Hitler and to guarantee the safety of the country.
> We repeat that the French Communists are and will be in the
> foremost ranks to crush the author of this criminal outrage against
> peace. The Communist deputies who can be called up, headed
> by Maurice Thorez, have rejoined their military companies. All
> are obeying the double duty of defeating Fascism and saving the
> liberties of our country.[14]

Auguste Lecoeur, an active Communist before and during the

---

12  Lefeuvre, p. 16.
13  French News Service, *Inside France*, Vol. 1, No. 1 (New York, May 25, 1940), p. 11.
14  *Ibid.*, p. 12.

Resistance who was once near the pinnacle of the P.C.F. but was later deposed for his unorthodox tendencies, wrote in his personal memoirs about the patriotism of party members despite persecution following the pact:

> The French Communist party was persecuted, but her militants rejoined the first line at the front, where they were for their compatriots a magnificent example of good citizenship, of unselfishness, and of patriotic courage.[15]

The large mass of the French Communist workers remained bewildered by the development of August 23rd. Many of them promptly moved to neutral territory where they could safely await further information, while others began defecting from the party membership.[16]

On the other hand, certain segments of French Communist opinion defended the Russo-German pact. Two days following the accord, on August 25th, the last legal issue of *L'Humanité* explained:

> The differences of ideologies and of political systems must not and can not serve as an obstacle to the establishment of good neighborly relations between the two countries. The friendship of the people of the U.S.S.R. and the people of Germany, who have been driven back into a dead end by the enemies of Germany and the U.S.S.R., must henceforth obtain the indispensable conditions for development and expansion.[17]

This article was one of the reasons used buy the Daladier government for outlawing the Communist press. The Daladier ministry,

---

15   Auguste Lecoeur, *Le Partisan* (France, 1963), p. 163.
16   Rossi, *P.P.C.F.*, p. 2.
17   *L'Humanité*, August 25, 1939.

however, had been most unhappy about the singing of the Russo-German pact in the first place. Soviet Russia and Hitlerite Germany had seemed unlikely to agree on anything; indeed, as bitter enemies they had regularly denounced one another. Furthermore, military missions from England and France were in Moscow to form a tripartite pact with the Soviet Union against Nazi Germany. Léon Blum, in referring to the Russo-German pact, well represented the surprise of the French government when he said:

> It is truly an extraordinary event, almost unbelievable, and by such a blow we are moreover stunned. The surprise is double when we remember that the horror and hate of Communism are the very sentiments by which Hitler has pretended to justify his recent enterprises. . . . And for her side, Soviet Russia has unceasingly stirred up anti-fascist propaganda.[18]

"A generation more versed in ideology than in power politics was dumbfounded."[19] The pact was recognized as the signal for war. The Germans were reassured by it and invaded Poland on September 1st. On September 3rd, Great Britain and France declared war on Germany.

Meanwhile, Russia, acting under the secret clauses of the German-Soviet pact, moved into the eastern half of Poland two weeks after the German invasion. The territory they occupied was roughly equivalent to that lost to Poland in 1920.

Daladier, who himself was rabidly anti-Communist, now had sufficient reason to treat the P.C.F. as the scapegoat. On August 25th he outlawed the Communist press, *L'Humanité* and *Ce Soir*, the party's evening paper. The P.C.F. became the subject of an increasing persecution and was itself declared illegal a month later.

---

18  Léon Blum, *L'Histoire Jugera* (Montreal, 1943), p. 239.
19  R.R. Palmer, *A History of the Modern World* (New York, 1964), p. 826.

Many party militants, as well as less devoted followers, however, remained in an uncertain and troubled state of mind. Some had divided loyalties between France and the U.S.S.R., but those whose first allegiance was to the U.S.S.R., especially the leadership of the P.C.F., were just waiting for more precise orders from Moscow. These orders came on September 20th, when Raymond Guyot brought them back after a trip to Moscow.[20] Then, eight days later, the Russo-German non-aggression pact became a treaty of friendship. There was now no question as to which direction the party should follow. The P.C.F. denounced the war as "imperialist," attacked the government, and started a campaign for immediate peace. It was at this point that desertions from the higher ranks of the party assumed a mass character. The P.C.F. originally had sucked in like a sponge a vast strata of workers and intellectuals attracted by militant leftism. These people had been educated in the spirit of unquestioning devotion to Stalin, but not in the spirit of friendship with Hitler. Such an alliance meant large-scale revolt. During the weeks following the outbreak of war, no fewer than twenty-one of its seventy-two deputies in the parliament broke with the party. In small batches, each of them was driven toward rupture by a certain specific move of the party. One of the party's two senators, fifteen members of the Seine "conseil général" and a large number of Communist mayors and municipal representatives left the party. Only the politburo was not significantly affected.[21] Its only member to break with the party was Marcel Gitton, who proclaimed:

> What is this comedy which consists of calling the present war, until September 30th, a war for the defense of democracy, of liberties, and of national independence and, dating from

20   Rossi, *P.C.F.*, p. 47.
21   Franz Borkenau, *European Communism* (London, 1953), p. 297.

October 1st, of styling it an imperialistic war? Why, if that is true did [we] vote 96 billion for the war on September 2nd?[22]

It is easy to understand why Gitton felt as he did, but such an attitude was not acceptable for a P.C.F. militant from whom an unswerving loyalty to Soviet directives was expected.

---

22   French News Service, Vol. 1, No. 1 (May 25, 1940), p. 12.

# Chapter II

# Second Stage

## ADJUSTMENT

Thus, in October 1939, the French Communist party entered the second stage of its role in the Second World War. Following the new line set by Moscow, the P.C.F. took an open stand against the war. In the same month, a pamphlet was received containing an article by Dimitrov, the Secretary of the Comintern. He proclaimed that "a courageous and relentless struggle against the war is the only legitimate policy." "The task of the hour," he added, "is to mobilize the masses against the war, in order that it might be brought to a speedy end."[23] This put an end to any remaining hesitations of the French party leaders. In an introduction to the pamphlet containing Dimitrov's article, they emphasized that the Secretary of the Comintern had clearly shown that it was the worker's duty to wage a fearless fight against the imperialist war. The party took up the Dimitrov thesis on every possible occasion.

To the party leadership it seemed entirely proper that one of their first acts in implementing the new policy should concern the highest matters of world diplomacy. On October 1st, after violent discussions within the Communist parliamentary group, where foreign affairs experts Gabriel Péri and Reynaud-Jean eliminated certain passages judged too provocative, Florimond Bonti and A. Ramette, in the name of the party's parliamentary

---

23   S. M. Osgood, *The Fall of France* (U.S.A., 1965), pp. 25–6.

group, submitted a letter to speaker Herriot, requesting an immediate convocation of the Chamber for the purpose of discussing a peace officer. "France will find herself at this very moment in the presence of peace proposals,"[24] ran the first sentence. Since no such proposals had been made, the statement was quite surprising. When the proposals did come a week later from Hitler in the form of a request to terminate hostilities on the basis of accepting the destruction of Poland, many Chamber members believed that the P.C.F. had already become the instrument of Hitlerite Germany. Although this was not the case—the P.C.F. took orders only from Moscow—the French Communists, in advance of the joint Hitler-Stalin request to let down Poland, were being used as a vanguard to start a mass campaign in favor of this diplomatic move.[25]

The Herriot letter was cushioned in courteous terms, due to the protests of Péri and Reynaud-Jean, but in a few days decorum no longer seemed in order. The P.C.F. aggressively and convincingly demonstrated the path of action it was to follow. First of all, on October 4th, Maurice Thorez deserted the army. As Secretary-General of the party, Thorez did what was expected, after the arrival of the new party line from Moscow. His desertion marked an open break of the party with the French Government only a few weeks after the opening of hostilities.[26] At that time Thorez, in addressing himself to the workers, the peasants, and the soldiers, declared that their

> duty is to organize everywhere the struggle of the masses against the imperialist war, for the purpose of peace and for the purpose of getting rid of the Daladier government which has no other

24    Borkenau, p. 300.
25    *Ibid.*
26    Rossi, *L.C.F.* p. 67.

preoccupation than that of fighting the working class and the country of victorious socialism.[27]

After Thorez's desertion, thousands of copies of tracts and underground papers came out explaining that he had deserted because this was an imperialist war, a war against the people. Thorez's action was an invitation to every soldier to desert, and since so many soldiers came for the working class and were tiring of the endless waiting of the "Phoney War" the temptation was very strong indeed. It is little wonder that the Daladier government stepped up their repressive measures and acts of persecution. Daladier gave his justification for the repression: "The violence and the intransigence of the Party has paralyzed my action."[28] It was falsely pretended by the P.C.F. for a short while that Thorez was conducting the underground struggle from within France. Actually, the Secretary-General had slipped into Belgium, where he remained until the end of 1939. He then passed into Switzerland, and by the beginning of the summer of 1940, he had arrived in Moscow, where he was to remain for the rest of the war under the false name of Ivanov.

The leadership of the illegal center of the P.C.F. was then taken over by Benoit Frachon. With him at the top was Jacques Duclos, the Secretary of the Central Committee. Deputies Ramette, Monmousseair, Fajon, Guyot, Péri, and Sémard were other upper echelon leaders of the P.C.F. who took part in the underground leadership of the party. André Marty, another prominent leader of the P.C.F., chose the part of safety and went to Moscow, where he sent back statements raving with hatred of his country.[29]

The Daladier government, by outlawing the Communist press

27   Maurice Thorez, *Oeuvres*, Book V, Vol. 19 (Paris, 1959), p. 9.
28   Gérald Walter, *Histoire du Parti Communiste Francais* (Paris, 1948), p. 341.
29   Borkenau, p. 302.

on August 25th and the P.C.F. on September 27th, had hoped to weaken greatly the power and influence of the Communist party over the people. According to Atkinson:

> Without desiring it, the government could not possibly have done the Party a better service. The Party was relieved of the impossible position of defending, in its extensive public press, the Russo-German pact, and of urging that France break with "imperialist" Britain and sue for peace with Germany through the good offices of the Soviet Union. Indeed, the Communist clandestine press took exactly this position, but, fortunately for the future of the French party, dissemination was necessarily restricted.[30]

Thus it seems that the Daladier government handled the whole matter with a great lack of tact and discrimination. The French working class had been adamantly opposed to Hitlerian fascism from the very beginning. Stalin's accord with Hitler originally seemed to many workers to be a "compromise with the devil." The effect of the persecution by Daladier, however, was to make these workers more sympathetic to the new party line. Werth agrees in adding:

> Had the Communist leaders been given enough freedom to defend Stalin, they might have made themselves very unpopular with the workers, who would have swung round in favor of the war. But all this persecution aroused in them feelings of party loyalty; and their attitude to the war became increasingly morose and skeptical. Thus the anti-Nazi working class, which might conceivably have remained anti-Nazi in spite of the Stalin-Hitler pact, became pacifist.[31]

---

30  Littleton B. Atkinson, *Communist Influence on French Rearmament* (Maxwell Air Force Base, Alabama, 1955), p. 1.

31  Werth, p. 346.

Although it is true that the persecution definitely made the French workers more sympathetic to the new pacifist line of the party, Werth's implication that the anti-Nazism of the working class somehow, in response to the persecution, became pacifism overnight seems a bit exaggerated. This is to ignore the fact that there was a strong tide of pacifism inherent in the French working class. Too many of its members still had unpleasant memories of the deaths of their fathers, brothers, and husbands in the first World War. Rossi substantiates this point in discussing the France of Autumn 1939:

> France is a this time fundamentally pacifist in its outlook: French opinion makes no sense of the "phoney war," and this means that the new Communist line is more congenial to the country's mood than the old one, and because more congenial it disposes people to overlook its inconsistency with the old one. These points can hardly be overemphasized. The contradiction between the two lines would perhaps prove fatal to the Party at this time if the discussion were projected on the level of intense patriotism, but no one forces it up to that level.[32]

Although the new Communist line in support of the Russo-German pact seemed unpatriotic to many workers, the pacifist message of the P.C.F. had a definite appeal to the many who wished to avoid bloodshed. This appeal was strengthened, again unwittingly, by the Daladier government as repressive measures against the P.C.F. increased following the letter to Herriot and the desertion of Thorez. From October 8th onwards, Communist deputies of civilian status were arrested, while those of military status were left alone. Several of them, and primarily Duclos, had already gone underground. On November 30th, when the Chamber was meeting

---

32   Rossi, *P.P.C.F.*, p. 6.

again, Florimond Bonté was sent by the party to read a provocative declaration; he was prevented from doing so and was arrested
on leaving the Chamber. Following this, the Chamber voted the
lifting of the Communists' parliamentary immunity. At the next
sitting of the Chamber, on January 9, 1940, four mobilized communist deputies appeared with a similar declaration. The Chamber
reacted by voting the unseating of all Communist deputies. Thus
the last link with legality was broken; the thirty-four Communist
deputies found themselves under arrest. Of the remaining seven-
teen (twenty-one had left the party), most were underground and
a few in the forces.[33]

Several months later, in March and April of 1940, the French
Communist deputies were put on trial. Although the deputies
insisted that their arrests and trials were illegal, since they were
the legally elected representatives of the people, they had little
chance. They were looked upon as traitors by the other deputies,
who unanimously voted against them. Thus, on April 3, 1940, the
3rd Military Tribunal of Paris pronounced the sentences against the
deputies of the P.C.F. Tried in their absence and receiving sentences
of five years imprisonment and fines of 5,000 francs were such
"bigwigs" as Thorez, Duclos, Monmousseau, Péri, Ramette, and
Tillon. Receiving sentences of five years and fines of 4,000 francs
were all of the arrested deputies, including Bonté, as well as other
non-deputy leaders of the P.C.F.[34]

## REORGANIZATION

The party was now faced with the situation of building up its
underground machine. This it did with surprising success. First
it was necessary to dissolve all overt groups and to reorganize the

33   Borkenau, p. 302.
34   André Marty, *The Trial of French Communist Deputies* (London, 1941),
       *passim.*

party structure. This had to be done from the top downwards. Regional and local committees were reconstituted and it was they who supervised the reconstruction of the ordinary membership by groups of three, selecting those they thought politically reliable and psychologically fit. This reorganization from above involved more than just a technical reconstruction. It also consisted of a large-scale purge which included a profound reshuffling of the basis of the party. Without the dropping of all "unreliable" elements, a policy of wholesale betrayal of the country could not have been carried through by a party which, only weeks before, had shared the ideology of the Popular Front.[35] Thus a merciless campaign against dissidents paralleled the reconstruction. It attempted to smear their personal characters and threatened them with vengeance. Attempts were made upon the lives of many of the dissidents.[36] One successful attempt was the murder of Gitton by Communists on September 4, 1940.

Simultaneously, the party attempted, though with less success, to reconstruct its trade union position underground. On September 18, 1939, immediately after the Russian invasion of Poland, the non-Communist majority of the national board of the Conféderation Général du Travail (C.G.T.) broke with the Communists. The expulsion of all those "unwilling or unable" to condemn the Nazi-Soviet Pact was ordered, and a reconstruction was started of all the unions previously under Communist leadership.[37] There were two reasons for this decision. First of all, co-operation between patriots and open traitors was out of the question. Secondly, any other method would have left the Communists in charge of large mass organizations that would have limited government repression. The C.G.T. was also hurt by this decision

---

35  Borkenau, p. 302.
36  A list of these attempts can be found on Rossi, *P.P.C.F.*, pp. 443–444.
37  Val R. Lorwin, *The French Labor Movement* (Cambridge, Mass., 1954).

as the Communists had controlled almost the whole Paris region, as well as many other important unions. The P.C.F. was not able to reconstruct effectively the unions underground. These clandestine unions, due to the severe repressive measures, never amounted to more than just "Communists active in a certain industry" until the outbreak of the war between Russia and Germany.[38] The Communists were quite naturally concerned about their relationship to the C.G.T. and the trade unions. Although the prestige of the P.C.F. in the trade unions suffered during the second stage of the party's wartime role, it was regained and heightened after the Germans had attacked the U.S.S.R. The P.C.F. had suddenly become quite patriotic. The Communists, however, regarded the trade unions as only a mere appendage of the party—as the most important of the "mass" organizations that the party needed to control. This control could be exercised through the indirect method of infiltration or the direct method of open sponsorship.[39] It was contrary to the traditions of the French trade unions to accept any subservient position to a political party; yet the number of Communists who were members of the C.G.T. gave the P.C.F. a significant advantage in this push for control.

Although many of the broader organizational plans of the party failed in the first several months of its clandestine existence, due to the persecutions, the organizational core of the P.C.F. remained unaffected. The French police succeeded from time to time in finding and catching a Communist group. For the most part, however, in contrast to the later efforts of the Gestapo, the work of the French police was very inefficient. Threats had little effect on the situation. In March 1940, when Daladier was replaced by Reynaud as Premier, a law was passed which, under certain conditions, made the continuation of Communist activities a capital

38  Borkenau, p. 303.
39  Rossi, *P.P.C.F.*, p. 248.

offense. Yet not a single execution took place under that law until the fall of France, and the empty gesture backfired. The number of Communists underground was small in the first few months of the second stage, but this number multiplied as the war became less and less popular.

## Propaganda

The Communist propaganda during this "phony war" period was one of the most significant and influential tools employed by the P.C.F. for obtaining its objectives. These objectives, which were primarily sabotage of the French war effort and overthrow of the present government, were greatly aided by the constant deluge of P.C.F. propaganda. The party aimed, by inundating as many people as possible, especially workers, with its tracts, journals and newspapers, to publicize the logic of their line and gain a larger following. In a tract Aux Membres du P.C.F., Thorez and Duclos reported that, as a result of the party's campaign, "propaganda against the war is reaching all segments of the working class, in factories, in the fields, and even in the trenches."[40] In its February issue of *Peuple de France*, the party urged "the formation of a united front of all workers, under the banner of the struggle against the imperialist war, against the Daladier government, and for peace."[41] The bi-weekly central organ of the Communist party, *L'Humanité*, led the way in its lambasting of the government and the capitalist war. In doing so, it set the tone of much of what appeared in other publications. Though highly partial, *L'Humanité* also attempted to substantiate logically the points it made. One of the earliest clandestine issues of the central organ proclaimed:

40    Maurice Thorez and Jacques Duclos, Letter addressed in the name of the Central Committee, February 1940; reproduced in Rossi, *L.C.F.*, Plate XX.
41    *Peuple de France*, February 1940; reproduced in Rossi, *L.C.F.*, Plates XXI and XXII.

Yes, the Communists denounce the present war as a war of capitalist brigands who are disputing territories and profits while in the process of massacring the people. . . . The proof that our government is waging an imperialist war is the fact that it is the instrument of the bankers and industrialists of the Committee of Forges who are the real masters of our country. It is that little fistful of men who comprise the financial oligarchy, who are imposing their wishes on the people, who are ordering the arrest of Communist deputies and honest militant syndicalists and obtaining the destruction of social laws while they accumulate their benefits in the misery of the people.[42]

Such reasoning made much sense to the average working-class reader, and there were very many such readers. On the back of the same issue, the workers were reminded that:

Because of the financial drain on the French government for war preparation, workers find that 60 hours of work a week are bringing them the same income that only 40 hours of work a week had given them previously. This extra money is going to the capitalist pockets of the Daladier government.[43]

Many workers and farmers, especially those who were forced to leave their wives and children at home while they impatiently waited on the front lines during the "Drole de guerre," were very hard hit by the tax burden. There was a 25 percent war tax on anything above 400 francs a week. The remainder of this was a 4 percent social insurance tax and a 2 percent extraordinary contribution tax. Then the remainder of that was hit by a 15 percent Retenue

---

42  *L'Humanité*, October 30, 1939.
43  *Ibid.*

tax.[44] Added to this heavy tax was the fact that, as of November 1, 1939, many workers were required to work extra hours at only 60 percent of their normal salary.[45] Thus it is easy to see how the P.C.F. was able to attract an increasingly sympathetic following among the French working class, a large number of whom had originally opposed the P.C.F. because of the party's anti-war stand following the Russo-German pact.

Although conditions such as the burden of the war taxation gave fuel to the Communist propaganda, the P.C.F. owed much of its increasingly sympathetic following to the good job accomplished by its propaganda. "Propaganda," proclaimed *La Vie du Parti*, "must occupy a prominent place in the activities of all party organizations."[46] Through its propaganda, the party called for the rallying of all progressive forces against the reactionaries of France "to bring the war to an end, to make peace."[47] The organizing of this struggle was the purpose of every tract and journal put out and circulated by the party. The party boasted that it "alone" was in opposition to the war,[48] and the leaders actually reminded the German authorities and the Vichy government of that fact when they attempted to gain their good will after the Armistice.

One of the main efforts of the nationwide campaign of the party during the first several months of 1940 was to win over the army. Since there was very little military activity in the overwhelming majority of sectors until May 10, 1940, many soldiers did not live apart from the population at large. The daily contact between civilian and soldier in the billeting areas, and the frequent leaves of soldiers to visit family and friends resulted in a continuing dialogue and an

44   *Ibid.*
45   *L'Humanité*, November 3, 1939.
46   *La Vie du Parti*, September 1940, p. 6, cited in Rossi, *P.P.C.F.*, p. 185.
47   Rossi, *L.C.F.*, p. 204.
48   *L'Humanité*, November 10, 1939.

exchange of views, of impressions, of complaints, and of information and, as was often the case, misinformation. Consequently, the outlook at the front came to reflect the prevailing sentiment at home. Thus, the morale of the army was very sensitive to the currents of French public opinion. From this situation the P.C.F. hoped to derive much benefit.

Hence, the propagandizing of the army became an essential activity for party militants. As Thorez declared, "The Communists have a clear duty to perform among the soldiers."[49] Recipients of the first issue of clandestine *L'Humanité* were urged to send it on to a friend in the armed forces. Thus it was hoped that the paper would pass from hand to hand, bringing the good word to the soldier in the trenches.

Leaders of the P.C.F. realized that their campaign would be blunted if the soldiers became isolated behind a wall of military discipline. Thus the party constantly reminded them that, even though they wore uniforms, they were free men, citizens, and members of the working class. In February 1940, *Peuple de France* proclaimed:

> Soldiers, remember that you are first and foremost workers,
> peasants, and laborers, whose interests are opposed to the goals
> of the men who are forcing you to fight.[50]

The Communists were so effective in gaining support for their action that they even got wives to write their soldier-husbands telling them about how bad conditions were back home. Likewise, soldiers were encouraged to demand that "their families be respected and

---

49   Rossi, *L.C.F.*, p. 206.
50   *Peuple de France*, February 1940, reproduced in Rossi, *L.C.F.*, Plates XXI
     and XXII.

provided for."[51] In such a way the propaganda of the P.C.F. helped to spread a feeling of widespread discontent

> "in factories, in the streets, among women waiting in long lines to buy oil or coffee, among soldiers wives in line to collect a meager allowance, and among soldiers who had become aware of what was really going on back home, and wanted peace."[52]

Much more than discontent, however, resulted from the Communist propaganda machine. When the P.C.F. hinted in its newspapers, tracts, and journals, of the desirability of desertion, there were real desertions. By prompting in its literature the sabotage of war production, the party instigated real acts of sabotage. According to Borkenau,

> a frighteningly large part of the armaments issuing from the Paris factories whose workers were under Communist influence were duds, or worse, were sabotaged so as to produce mortal accidents.[53]

He adds that

> It is difficult to assess quantitatively the effects of Communist propaganda for desertion, fraternization with the enemy, and throwing away one's arms. But the [French] generals were convinced that Communist propaganda was a major factor in the rapid collapse of the army.[54]

---

51   *Ibid.*
52   *La Voix des Usines*, No. 1 (April 1941), cited in Rossi, *L.C.F.*, p. 207.
53   Borkenau, p. 304.
54   *Ibid.*

## INDUSTRIAL PLANTS

The party's principal field of activity continued to be the industrial plants, largely because there were many connections between the army and the factories. Furthermore, a number of the industrial workers were loyal members of the P.C.F. Since many skilled workers in the army were sent back to war plants from time to time on temporary assignments, there was a steady channel of communications between the factories and the front, and this the P.C.F. exploited. The delivery of war materials, besides providing contacts between soldiers and workers, gave the P.C.F. a chance to send bundles of tracts and newspapers to the front line. Most importantly, however, the industrial plant was vital to the production of war materials. Any Communist success at hampering production would have automatic repercussions at the front. Thus the P.C.F. could exercise a direct influence on the war, the outcome of which could be largely determined in the factories. The Finnish War, during which the French sent supplies to the Finns for use against the U.S.S.R., had led to the first acts of sabotage, but this was only the beginning. Subsequently, the party urged all workers:

> Use all appropriate means, use your intelligence and technical knowledge, to prevent, delay, and sabotage the production of war material.[55]

With such encouragement acts of sabotage greatly increased. One eighteen-year-old member of the Jeunesses Communistes, Roger Rambaud, was a skilled aircraft mechanic. He had begun by sabotaging no more than two or three aircraft engines a day. However, with a little urging he was sabotaging twenty engines a

---

55   A tract titled *Daladier, Chamberlain, Mussolini, Franco* & Pie XII, reproduced in Rossi, *L.C.F.*, Place XXIII.

day. Not surprisingly, Rambaud, like many other Communists, was arrested, tried, and executed for his activities.[56] In its effort to make the war as "unpopular" as possible, the P.C.F. justified its extreme policies and tactics with the slogan: "An hour lost for war production is an hour gained for the revolution."[57]

## THE FALL OF FRANCE

The six-week German blitzkrieg over France in May-June of 1940 may have been aided somewhat by the sabotage and propaganda tactics of the P.C.F. But the catastrophic French defeat was much more the result of a long political, military and social crisis that had been deteriorating since 1934. Be that as it may, the impending French defeat was to cause a wavering in the Communist propaganda line by May 1940. Previously, the P.C.F. had sided openly and unreservedly with Hitler, but as the fighting touched French soil, such an attitude was no longer viable. The P.C.F. started talking anti-Nazism again, though in a very special manner. The first number of *L'Humanité* to be issued after the campaign had begun on May 15, 1940:

For the workers and soldiers, the Anglo-French imperialism, which is responsible for the war...is not more attractive simply because it is fighting with an equally hateful imperialism. When two gangsters fight, decent people have no occasion to help one of them under the pretext that he has been dealt an illegal blow. They try on the contrary to profit from the situation so as to put them both out of any possibility to do harm. Everyone will try to beat down the one who is most easily accessible to him. . . . While the German people fight against its bourgeoisie, we must fight against our own bourgeoisie in France, for it is the one we

---

56   Rossi, *L.C.F.*, pp. 209 and 218.
57   Bulletin d'Information Ouvriére, No. 3 (March 15, 1940), cited in Rossi, *L.C.F.*, p. 210.

can weaken by our action in the factories and in the army.[58]

Since the German Communists were doing very little at that time to hamper German war effort, it seems likely that the principle motivation for this slight change of line was to gain an alibi for the central propaganda campaign of the moment—namely, that of weakening and defeating the French resistance to the Germans. This seeming ruse would make the P.C.F. appear not so much anti-French as anti-imperialist-bourgeoisie. For the Communists, who were planning an overthrow of the Republic during these dark days, this was a good ploy. An attempt to overthrow seemed eminent when, on June 18th, the P.C.F. distributed a pamphlet in Bordeaux urging their leaders to "demand the immediate arrest of the traitors and the establishment of a genuinely popular government, resting upon mass support." Such a government, they pointed out, "will of course free the workers now in jail, remove the ban on the Communist party, and press the struggle against the fascism of Hitler and the two hundred families."[59] According to Borkenau, the politburo of the P.C.F. had little if any control with the Soviet Union during these hectic Bordeaux days, and therefore it must be assumed that this change of line was entirely a function of the French Communists' bid for power.[60] In any case, this effort at Bordeaux proved to be too complicated and chaotic, and the party leaders soon realized that this struggle for power could only be led from Paris.

## OCCUPATION

As the Armistice was concluded and the Germans moved into France as the occupying power, the P.C.F., in liason with representatives of the U.S.S.R., worked out a concrete plan of action based

---

58  *L'Humanité*
59  *Appel au Peuple de France*, published as pamphlet (Bordeaux, June 18, 1940), cited in Rossi, *P.F.C.F.,* p. 11.
60  Borkenau, p. 307.

on a new appraisal of the situation at home and abroad. The broad outlines of this plan, certain elements of which had appeared in previous publications, could be recognized in *L'Humanité* of July 1, 1940, and in the Manifesto to the People of France, a document from the party's Central Committee. This plan was to remain the party line for the remaining months up until the outbreak of the war between Germany and the U.S.S.R., and on June 22, 1941, only slight but unavoidable alterations were necessary. Some of the major emphases of the program are as follows:

A. We are free to face with a genuine revolutionary situation. Because France has fallen, and become the two opposing "capitalist" blocs will wear themselves out as the war continues, the order of the day for the French Communists is the conquest of power.

B. The conquest of power is out of question unless peace is concluded with Germany within the immediate future. Only a Communist government can negotiate an early peace.

C. The Party's relations with the occupying power depend and will continue to depend, on the German-Soviet Pact. These relations are of such a character as to give the Party a relatively free hand in the present revolutionary situation, and will in no way jeopardize the Party's good name.

D. The Party will be effective only as it succeeds in tying itself to the broad masses of the population.[61]

The French Communists hoped to accomplish a revolution "à la mode Bolshevik de 1917." The first condition, however, for the revolution was to be the conclusion of peace with Germany. Friendly relations with the occupying power had to be established. The P.C.F. wanted to reach the same kind of "modus vivendi" with

---

61   *L'Humanité*, July 1, 1940. p. 1

the occupier that the Soviets and Germans had adopted in signing their pact. By doing so, the party hoped to facilitate its eventual "putsch."

This policy of cooperation with the occupation authorities did pay some dividends. In a secret set of instructions sent to all party members around the beginning of July, the politburo pointed out that in the Nazi-controlled press appearing in the occupied zone

> not a single paper directly attacks the Communists party. They never seem to make concessions to our political program, thus justifying it. The P.C.F. is no longer completely illegal. It is half legal. Thus, the distributors of our leaflets, when arrested by the French police are released the day after through the intervention of the (German) kommandantur. The political prisoners in the occupied regions, with the exception of all the deputies, have been liberated by the German troops, together with the members of the fifth column. . . . To sum up, the immediate objective is the struggle for the lifting of the ban upon the party.[62]

While seeking this objective, the P.C.F. entered wholeheartedly into collaboration with the Germans. Collaboration and fraternization were the keywords in *L'Humanité* of Bastille Day 1940, which said:

> French Workers and German soldiers: It is especially comforting in this unhappy time to see numerous Parisian workers mixing in friendship with German soldiers, be it in the street or at the corner newspaper stand.[63]

The P.C.F., in its propaganda, continued to emphasize its

---

62  Borkenau, pp. 308–9.
63  *L'Humanité*, July 14, 1940.

friendship with the German occupier. In so doing it expected the Germans to reciprocate by authorizing the legalization of the P.C.F. and its clandestine press. The P.C.F. also hoped to gain a reinstallation of the elected Communists now in jail, but it was hoping unreasonably when it asked the German authorities to join the Communists in a "Front unique" against all the parties which had opposed the Germans in the war.[64]

The Germans had reason to court the Communists, too, since they believed that the P.C.F., with its organization, was the key to the French masses. It was necessary for the Nazi authorities to carry the masses in order to control France. The P.C.F., however, came to direct increasingly their fire against the Vichy government of Pétain and Laval. And the Vichy authorities reciprocated with measures of repression against the P.C.F. Unfortunately, for the Communists, the Germans were closer to Vichy than to the P.C.F. As Hitler's stand-by in France, the Vichy government worked hand in hand with the Germans. Consequently, the P.C.F. at this time could not be sure just where it stood with the Nazi authorities, whose toleration could not be sure just where it stood with the Nazi authorities, whose toleration could not be counted on indefinitely. In late September a secret party directive stated:

> . . . We must, while pressing forward as energetically as possible with our underground activity against capitalism, act with skill and caution. We must not give ourselves illusions about the toleration we enjoy: it might, from one day to the next, be transformed into repression.[65]

And so it did. From October onwards, the Germans, even in

---

64    Lefeuvre, *La Politique Communiste*, pp. 25–6.
65    *Les Tâches du Parti pour septembre-octobre*, published as a pamphlet, August 1940, reproduced in Rossi, *P.P.C.F.*, pp. 399–402.

the occupied zone, assisted the French police in persecuting the Communists. Though the Gestapo initially left the P.C.F. alone, following this policy reversal, it, too, eventually started "cooperating" with the Vichy police.

Accordingly, the politburo in December ordered a complete return to underground methods, the party having lost its semi-legality. The P.C.F. refrained from any direct attack upon the occupying power. Instead it attacked the Vichy government for its collaboration.

During the first several months of 1941, the acts of repression against the P.C.F. increased. Many Communists were rounded up and placed in internment camps. At Clermont-Ferrand, a "cell" leader was sentenced to twenty years at forced labor.[66] On May 22nd, Gabriel Péri, one of the top Communist leaders, was captured in the home of a friend in a Paris suburb.[67]

Meanwhile, members of the P.C.F. were becoming increasingly divided on how to react to the German occupier. The politburo, loyal as always to Soviet directives, tried to tone down growing anti-Nazi tendencies in the ranks. From the beginning of the hostilities with Germany, a number of less-devoted worker-Communists had strayed from the outbreak of the war, and with the consequent defeat and occupation by the Germans, additional Communists broke with the party. In the case of most of these members they were not yet the devoted party militants which the politburo demanded. They were not yet willing to place the fatherland of workers, the U.S.S.R., over their native land. Some of these Nazi-haters went so far as to resist openly against the German occupier.

There was a small French Resistance movement against the Nazis at work before June 22, 1941. The Communist party organization, however, would have nothing to do with it. This attitude was not

---

66  *New York Times*, February 2, 1941, p.7.
67  *Ibid.*, May 23, 1941, p. 5.

popular among many P.C.F. militants. Consequently, there were many individual deviations from it. Although the party leadership did not waver in its stand, the increasing alienation felt by certain members toward the Germans caused the anti-Nazi and pro-Resistance sentiment to grow.

This anti-Nazi sentiment in the Communist ranks did swell considerably in 1941, especially after the German offensive in the Balkans. The party's clandestine press started using anti-Nazi language. In connection with the attack upon Yugoslavia, *L'Humanité* of April 12, 1941, spoke of the "Berlin incendiaries." The miner's strike in northern France near the end of May 1941 was another source of friction between the P.C.F. and the Germans. The mass arrests made by the Gestapo were severely criticized by the P.C.F.[68]

The leadership of the P.C.F., with reminders from the U.S.S.R., tried to control this growing anti-Nazi feeling, yet the Soviet directives to this affect became increasingly weaker as the belligerent actions of the Third Reich were giving the Soviets cause for misgivings and apprehension about German intentions.

---

68    Borkenau, p. 313.

# Part Two

# Resolve:
# Third Stage

JUNE 22, 1941–LIBERATION, AUGUST 1944

# Chapter III

# Reversal

The German attack on the Soviet Union June 22, 1941, ended the recent divisions in Communist ranks. Doubt and misgiving disappeared as a unified P. C. F. entered the third stage of its wartime role, which was actually the only stage involving its active resistance against the Nazis. The Nazi attack made it possible for members of the French Communist party to be good Frenchmen as well as militant Communists. "In attacking the U.S.S.R.," said the P.C.F. leader Duclos, "Germany not only roused the anger of the workers, she opened up a new horizon to the French people."[69]

## New Horizon

Into this new horizon and into the forefront of the Resistance the Communists moved with vigor. By their unyielding courage, their devotion, and their ceaseless activity in spite of terrible persecution, the Communists came to earn every right to the title they proudly claimed and were later to exploit—"le parti des fusillés" (the party of the executed).

The P.C.F. had a few significant advantages over other Resistance parties and groups that were forming or had just recently formed organizations. First of all, it had a year's start as an underground organization. The Communists began their clandestine existence in September of 1939, following the Russo-German pact, whereas

---

69    Dorothy M. Pickles, *France Between the Republics* (London, 1946), p. 97.

the earliest other Resistance groups could start was the summer of 1940, following the fall of France. The Communists were also able to form their cadres and organize their local sections undisturbed by the Gestapo; the others were not so fortunate. Besides, the attitude of most Frenchmen following the fall of France was one of "attentisme"[70] (wait and see). Consequently, the numbers in non-communist organizations were initially very small. Even a year later, when Germany attacked the Soviet Union, the other Resistance réseaux (networks) still had small memberships and quite limited functions. Added to this longer experience of the P.C.F. as a clandestine organization were a discipline, a unity, and a coordination lacking in other Resistance groups. Furthermore, the Party already had at its disposal a small but efficient band of international party operatives whose whole existence was anonymous and subterranean. This restricted elite included organizers, tacticians, saboteurs, and assassins.[71] Thus the Communists were able to obtain, and later to maintain, a much higher degree of effectiveness in their efforts.

Following the outbreak of war between Russia and Germany, the Party leadership informed P.C.F. members that they were free until further notice to be as patriotic as the next guy—and more since, in the present situation, any difficulties created between the French and occupation authorities would be to the advantage of the U.S.S.R. Vie du Parti instructed P.C.F. members:

> In the present circumstances, no distinction can be drawn between the behavior of the Communists and that of any other patriot.[72]

The new battle cry of the party combined Communist and patriotic slogans: "Today if you are not for the U.S.S.R. then you

---

70   Interview with Henri Michel, Paris, June 29, 1967.
71   Blake Ehrlich, *Resistance: France, 1940–45* (New York, 1965), p. 56.
72   *Vie du Parti* (4th quarter, 1941), p. 14 as cited in Rossi, P.P.C.A., p. 103.

are against France; 1789–1793: The people hang traitors and drive out the foreigners, Frenchmen: Remember."[73]

Besides helping the U.S.S.R. by hurting Germany, this identification by the P.C.F. with French patriotism had an additional purpose. The P.C.F. hoped, by broadening the base of its National Front (the chief party apparatus), to reach into as many social, financial, and industrial groups as possible and obtain a representative French membership. The non-organized of other political beliefs could not prevail against the Party core which controlled the units.[74] This typical Communist-front tactic worked extremely well, and the P.C.F. hoped it would widen the launching pad for its post-war takeover.

Likewise, a number of Communists were able to infiltrate other Resistance groups. This was especially the case of those party members who had ignored the Pacifist line of the P.C.F. during the second stage, but put themselves under party orders when the turnabout came. Many of these members had joined the budding non-party resistance groups in their areas. Such non-Communist resistance réseaux were also joined by other party militants following the German attack of Russia. Although his intelligence reports were slow to assess the existence and the extent of the Communist "front" tactics, on the one hand, and the subversion on the other, Gen. de Gaulle recognized this fact in his Memoirs. Said he:

> So it was that, in the occupied zone, they (the P.C.F.) formed the Front National, a group that was purely patriotic in aspect, and the Francs-Tineurs et Partisans, a force that seemed intended only for the struggle against the Germans. So it was that into these they attracted many elements that were non-Communist but, from that very fact, might serve as cover for their designs. So it was that they camouflaged some of their own people and

---

73    Tract reproduced in Rossi, *La Guerre des Papillons*, Plate XIX, No. 7.
74    Interview with H. Michel, Paris, June 29, 1967.

pushed them into directing organs of all the other movements. So it was that they were soon to offer me their assistance, though never ceasing to mutter against the "de Gaulle myth."[75]

Both Communist groups were ready to take over for the P.C.F. when the opportunity came. "And it did come when, just before liberation, a number of curiously coincidental deaths and arrests of non-Communist leaders made vacancies in command in non-party organizations."[76]

At the same time, the communists were zealously maintaining their independence, both in policy and in action. In fact, during the first nine months following the outbreak of the Russo-German war, Communist relations with other parties or allied authorities were non-existent.[77] Of eleven contact missions sent by de Gaulle's Free French to the home country in 1941, the only one to remain unsuccessful was the one directed to the Communists. They "remained undiscoverable."[78]

Thus, the P.C.F. managed to maintain its independence from any other authority. Simultaneously, it broadened its base of support. The National Front declared that it would include everyone prepared to use "all available means" in achieving the following "common" objectives:

1. Prevent the German war machine from using French resources;

2. See to it that no French factories work for Hitler and at the same time back up the workers in their day-to-day struggles over grievances (the workers, in fighting for their own bread and that of their children, are serving the cause of France);

75 *The Complete War Memoirs of Charles de Gaulle* (New York, 1964), p. 268.
76 Ehrlich, p. 57.
77 Passy (pseud. for André Dewarrin), *Souvenirs, 2 e Bureau Londres* (Monte Carlo, 1947), p. 135.
78 Jacques Soustelle, *Envers et Contre Tout*, Vol. 1 (Paris, 1947), p. 311.

3. See to it that France's railroads shall not carry its national wealth and the products of its industry into Germany;

4. Organize peasant resistance against delivery of agricultural products to France's oppressors;

5. Organize the struggle against Hitler-Vichy repression (every National Front militant, atheist or believer, Radical or Communist must enjoy the benefits accruing from our common solidarity);

6. Assure wide distribution for such books and pamphlets, manifestos, and other documents as the National Front may wish to circulate, and at the same time systematically expose the lies of the enemy;

7. Stimulate and extend—in the teeth of the invader and his henchmen—the sentiment of patriotism and the will to fight for the liberation of France.[79]

With these aims in mind, the P.C.F., through its instrument, the National (Liberation) Front, greatly expanded the dimensions of its activity.

## ACTIVITY INCREASES

During the first year of the Russia war the party activity in the Vichy (unoccupied) zone consisted mainly of political, primarily propaganda, work, although there was a sprouting military resistance. In the occupied zone, the P.C.F. concentrated on military action the first year.[80] The first action groups were small shock units called OS (Special Organizations). The OS directed its efforts on sabotage and attacks against German army personnel. On August 15, 1941, there was a spread of arson directed mostly against arms plants and other war industries under German control. In Paris an important electrical parts plant that had important war orders was

---

79   *Cahiers du Bochévisme* (2nd and 3rd quarters, 1941), p. 32, as cited in Rossi, *P.P.C.F.*, p. 128.

80   Passy, *Souvenirs*, p. 135.

set afire. In Versailles, another "mystery" fire destroyed the Graff factories with a 2,500,000 franc loss.[81]

The Communists were immediately blamed, and rightly so, for these fires. Due to the arson and Communist-inspired riots in Paris, the Commander of the German armies of occupied France, General Heinrich von Stuelpnagel, announced that death would be the penalty for the slightest Communist activity in Paris. His notice added that anyone possessing a Communist tract must immediately turn it over to the nearest German military post. Failure to do so could result in a prison term of up to fifteen years.[82]

Despite these threats the Communists stepped up their activities. On August 23rd, a high German officer was assassinated.[83] And the "Guerre des Papillons" (war of tracts) continued as the Communists distributed tons of tracts daily, dumping them in mailboxes and hallways. On August 26th, a car drove up near the Orleans gate and three men pushed out a huge bail resembling cotton. One of them slashed the bail with a knife and a great quantity of tracts spilled out.[84] Such were the techniques employed by the Communists.

On the same day, in an interview with American journalists, Ferdinand de Brinon, Vichy envoy to Paris, reported that 100 cases of Communist sabotage against French railways had taken place since June 22, 1941.[85] Outraged, the German and French authorities sought to stem the tide of disorders by decreeing new death penalties for the failure to halt railway sabotage.[86] Communist hostages were summarily executed.

The repression was severe, the penalties were capital, but the risks were worth it, according to the P.C.F. Due to all of the disorders—the

81  *New York Times*, August 16, 1941, p. 4.
82  *Ibid.*
83  *Ibid.*, August 23, 1941, p. 1.
84  *Ibid.* August 26, 1941, pp. 1, 5.
85  *Ibid.*
86  *Ibid.*, August 27, 1941, p. 4.

arsons, the train derailments, the riots, the assassinations, the propaganda distribution, and the factory sabotage of German war material—the German high command, kept in constant anxiety, had to divert large numbers of soldiers from other areas where they were badly needed. In the Paris area alone approximately 20,000 German soldiers had to be assigned to help Paris police crush the rampant agitation.[87] Besides causing direct damage to the Germans in their sabotage activities, the P.C.F. reasoned that keeping such a large number of troops away from the battlefields could only hurt the German war effort.

## "Co-Escalation"

The Nazi authorities initially held the Communists and Jews responsible for all of their troubles. During one two-day period in August 1941, seven thousand members of these two groups were rounded up, following a seizure of four thousand in a previous raid.[88] Soon, however, the Communists were considered the lone culprit. While it is true that the P.C.F. was responsible for a large part of the disorder, they were often blamed for acts committed by other Resistance groups.

When the Germans started increasing the executions of Communists accused of terrorism and anti-German actions, the P.C.F. broadcasted that "for every one of their number executed, ten Germans will die."[89] This broadcast seemingly had little effect on the Nazis. Accordingly, the P.C.F. increased its assassination rate. As the escalation continued, fifty hostages, most of them Communists, were executed on October 22, 1941. Facing the firing squad, they yelled out: "Long live France! Long live the Soviet Union! Long live Stalin!"[90]

---

87    *Ibid.*, August 28, 1941, p. 8.
88    *Ibid.*, August 24, 1941, p. 28.
89    *Ibid.*, Sept. 8, 1941, p. 1.
90    Maurice Thorez, *Pour L'Union Le Front Francais* (Paris, 1947), p. 50.

# Chapter IV

# Consolidation

By 1942, the P.C.F. had greatly consolidated the areas of its activity and increased the influence it was exerting. The party had more members than any other Resistance organization and it had certainly become the most violent of all the Resistance groups. In the suburbs of Paris, the two top leaders of the P.C.F., Jacques Duclos and Benoit Frachon, maintained the party headquarters in a highly secret lodge. According to Jacques Fauvet, they were a "team of fidelity and solidarity."[91] They made all of the important decisions and shared the daily work. Duclos, the more political of the two, supervised the press and the propaganda. Frachon, a trade unionist, concerned himself more with questions of organization, material, and matters pertaining to trade unions. Both of them remained invisible to other party leaders for security reasons. Marcel Prenant, the Deputy-Commander of the Franc-Tineurs et Partisans Francais (FTP), the fighting wing of the National Front, was never allowed to see either of them, despite the great confidence that both had in him. The arrest of Prenant in 1944 justified this policy; the Nazi authorities had brutal torture methods for extracting information. Although most captured French Communists so treated held up inhumanly well, to the point of death in refusing to give information, the Party believed it unnecessary to run useless risks. Auguste Lecoeur was responsible for an "interregion" of

---

91  Jacques Fauvet, *Histoire du Parti Communiste Francais*. (Paris, 1965), p. 98.

six departments. Despite his important position, the only way he could communicate with the "Big Two" of the P.C.F. was through intermediaries. This vertical organization of the Party, considered highly essential during its legal, pre-war existence, was all the more necessary to insure security during the Resistance.[92]

## Structure and Security

Due to the increased volume and pace of the Party's activity, the P.C.F. decided to decentralize somewhat its resistance organization. In so doing, it hoped that a more immediate leadership might inspire greater effectiveness. Thus a delegation was installed by the P.C.F. for all of the southern (or unoccupied) zone at Lyon, which had quickly become by the end of 1942 the capital of the Resistance. Leon Mauvais, a forty-year old with the reputation of a "tough guy," was put in charge. Assisting him were Raymond Guyot and Gaston Monmousseau. France was divided into fourteen "interregions," nine for the northern zone and five for the southern zone. Each interregion contained several départments (or districts). At the base of the organization a return to groups of three was imposed upon party members. This was another security measure in the face of severe repression. "Three" was a less unwieldy and a more effective number for a group. This number was much safer, too, since only those leaders at the very top of the P.C.F. pyramid knew the whereabouts and activities of other three-man groups. Any contact between the different groups was absolutely forbidden. Instructions for prudence were continually renewed. Recruits who were too talkative or militants who were a bit careless had to mend their ways or be excluded from participation. A Communist released by the police became immediately suspect. The rule was hard but necessary. At all the echelons of the party—from the

---

92  Charles A. Micaud, *Communism and the French Left* (London, 1963), p. 79.

interregions, départmental federations, sections, and cells to the three-man groups—the training was severe,[93] for a weak link at any level in the hierarchy could prove disastrous to the most hotly pursued political group in wartime France.

Nonetheless, the party could not escape numerous arrests and cruel treatment. The P.C.F. did all it could to prevent such happenings; the party's rules for underground activity became the model for clandestinité.

## REGULATIONS

What were some of these measures employed by the P.C.F. for self-protection? One general rule was that no militant known to be a Communist before the war could participate in any underground activity without first adopting certain conditions. For instance, "he must never, for any reason whatever, go near any address that is known to the police in connection with him; since any such address is sure to be under surveillance."[94] Another rule applicable to any militant living at a known address and about to participate in an underground mission states that he must not only change his address but sever his relations with his family. A party pamphlet declared: "The militant called upon to choose between his family life and work for the party has an easy choice."[95] The party reasoned that it was better for a militant to be temporarily separated from his family than captured and sent a great distance away to a German labor camp. Another rule cautioned members against disclosing their identity to strangers and warned against indulging such frailties as vanity and curiosity. Conversation was to be kept to the minimum, especially with outsiders, and no unnecessary or indiscreet questions were to be asked of one another. No meetings

93 Fauvet, p. 99.
94 *Vie du Parti* (2nd quarter, 1941), p. 9, as cited in Rossi, *P.P.C.F.*, p. 251.
95 *Comment se défendre*, p. 10, as cited in Rossi, *P.P.C.F.*, p. 253.

could have more than three present or last longer than sixty minutes. Militants were expected to arrive at a rendezvous precisely on time ("arriving early attracts attention to you, arriving late exposes the comrade waiting on you"). Meeting places which might be under surveillance were avoided in place of those which police would be less likely to consider (theater lobbies, places in the country, or the seashore).[96] Any militant whose mission required him to make use of party document had to make sure that all information that could be useful to a policeman was in code. Were he to be stopped while on such a mission, every effort to destroy the papers had to be made, including chewing them up and swallowing them.[97] There were a multitude of other regulations concerning behavior, mode of dress and other matters for party militants. Strict adherence to these guidelines was a necessity as constant threats were being posed to the well-being of the militant and the security of the party by the Gestapo and Vichy police. Consequently, the regulations expounded in such pamphlets as Comment se défendre? and Soyons hardis, Soyons prudent and the quarterly Vie du Parti had to be known by heart by all party militants.

## FN Broadens Base

The year 1942 saw the National Front (FN) and its paramilitary auxiliary the F.T.P. gain a greater following and influence. The FN was the only Resistance movement which had widespread influence in both the occupied zone (under the leadership of Pierre Villon) and the unoccupied zone (led by Georges Marrane). Its ideology and propaganda were similar to that of the regular Party, if toned down a bit to include its broader following, and all of the command posts in the political and military branches were in the hands of leading Communists. The FN had been quite successful in attracting a

---

96   Soyons hardis, Soyons prudents, p. 3, as cited in Rossi, P.P.C.F., p. 253.
97   A. Rossi, P.P.C.F., p. 254.

cross-section of widely diverse political elements. It took delight in parading such names as François Mauriac, Monseigneur Chevrot, Georges Bidault, none of whom were Communist, and Frédéric Joliot-Curie, then a Socialist. They were all on the executive committee, but in name only. Many Frenchmen who would never have considered becoming members of the P.C.F. were attracted by such names and joined the FN. These Frenchmen, to be greatly differentiated from party militants, had their highest value in giving the FN a sufficiently patriotic visage to carry out certain actions which it could not otherwise have performed without being suspected of trying to seize power in France.[98]

## INCLUDES INTELLECTUALS

With its broad appeal, the "Front National" eventually attracted into its ranks a number of Communist and Socialist intellectuals, not to mention Catholic writers like Mauriac. At the same time, party intellectuals were active in the unoccupied zone in such non-front movements as Libération, led by Emmanuel d'Astier de la Vigerie (first a Gaullist but later a Communist), and in the coalition resistance groups, Mouvements Unis de Résistance (M.U.R.) and Mouvement de Libération Nationale (M.L.N.). The leader of the intellectual group (Groupes Francs) of the M.U.R. was a young Communist named Serge Asher, who organized the Resistance among students at Lyons.[99]

The principal Communist-controlled body was the Front National des Intellectuels, which in 1941 already included a number of well-known and influential intellectuals whose support was beneficial to the Party. Numerous specialist organizations were created within which the intellectuals were grouped into amicales

---

98    Alfred J. Rieber, *Stalin and the French Communist Party* (New York, 1962), pp. 60, 85–86.

99    David Caute, *Communism and the French Intellectuals* (New York, 1964).

(cells). Among the better known of such Communist controlled units located in the northern zone were the Front Nationale Universitaire, the Comité National des Juristes and the Front National des Arts. They were supported by clandestine papers and journals, such as *L'Université libre, L'École laique, La Médecine Francaise, L'Art Francais, Les Étoiles* and *Les Lettres Francaises*. All together, these bodies claimed 100,000 members by the end of the war.[100] Obviously, such a number was quite meaningful to the P.C.F. and its post-war designs.

Most effective and durable of these front organizations proved to be the Comité National des Ecrivains (C.N.E.), the majority of whose members had found the Communist attitude during the "Phony War" unsupportable, if not repugnant. Among the famous writers of the C.N.E. were Claude Bourdet, André Malraux, Albert Camus, and Jean-Paul Sartre. Sartre had attempted an early "rapprochement" with the Communist intellectuals in 1941 but was told that if he had been released as a prisoner of war by the Germans it must have been for services rendered. Early in 1943, however, he was invited to rejoin the C.N.E., with apologies for what had been said earlier.

The C.N.E.'s organ *Les Lettres Francaises* clandestines became one of the most influential and widely respected voices of the intellectual Resistance. This paper, like other clandestine papers and journals, played an important role in the Resistance by influencing the opinion of its readers against the Germans. Backed by the subsidiary "fronts" of the FN, these clandestine issues won much support for the French Communists.[101]

---

100  Georges Cognoit, *Les Intellectuels et la Renaissance Francaise* (Paris, 1945), p. 20.
101  Caute, pp. 150–51.

## THE F.T.P.

The Francs-Tireurs et Partisans, as the military arm of the FN, was also in the process of widening its influence. In March 1942, the F.T.P., having absorbed the earlier OS units, stepped up efforts to increase its military force. "Everywhere," *L'Humanité* proclaimed, "patriots must constitute groups of Francs-Tireurs et Partisans to make life miserable for the occupying forces, and must carry on a guerrilla war which, from the armistice line to the farthest corners of the country, will give no respite to the enemy."[102]

The organization of the F.T.P. (known also as Communist maquis) was based on a fighting group composed of two detachments. As was the case with regular party units, each F.T.P. detachment consisted of three men. One of the two detachments was led by the group advisor; the other by the deputy group adviser. Three groups formed a platoon, three platoons a company, and three companies a battalion. In suitable locations, battalions were combined and their action coordinated on a departmental scale by an executive committee of three men. In turn, the departmental executive was subordinated to the interdepartmental committee of three. At the top of this military pyramid was the National Military Committee, which was itself divided into three sections—intelligence, medical, and arms and munitions—and it also published its own newspaper *France d'abord*. This committee was headed by F.T.P. commander Charles Tillon and his deputy Marcel Prenant.[103]

The F.T.P. displayed an uncompromising attitude in its struggle against the enemy. Many Resistance groups, however, paid attention to Gaullist advice and took a more cautious stance. The fiercely independent F.T.P., to the contrary, avoided Gaullist control, except when political expediency suggested it. In fact, de Gaulle was

---

102 *L'Humanité*, special number (March 1942).
103 Rieber, pp. 83–4.

unable to make contact with the F.T.P. until May 1942 when his agent Colonel Rémy finally succeeded in doing so. The lack of compromise by the F.T.P. with de Gaulle was partially due to the question of which resistance tactics were the best to use against the Nazis: to attack or wait?

The F.T.P. maintained that violence was the only way, especially in cities, to rip open the Nazi shroud of fear enveloping the populace, to demonstrate beyond doubt that the conquerors were vulnerable and that armed resistance and eventual victory were possible. Another argument, already stated,[104] was that the large number of German troops required to keep order in France diverted much-needed manpower from the multi-fronted German war effort. The Party hoped, in using the F.T.P. to pressure the occupying power, to hold in the French theater large numbers of German soldiers who might otherwise take part in the drive toward Moscow.

A third reason given by the F.T.P. in favor of the killing and destroying was that the enemy would never again feel secure in occupied territory. Proclaimed Notre Jeunesse:

> We must blow up bridges, destroy highways and telephone lines, and set fire to fuel tanks. We must make the situation in the occupied countries intolerable for the enemy; we must harass him at every turn, strike him down at every opportunity, abort his every plan.[105]

Fourthly, as each fallen enemy was stripped of his weapons, the Resistance would arm itself.

The Gaullists countered by saying that the Nazis were sure to

---

104 *Supra*, p. 43.
105 *Notre Jeunesse* (September–October 1941), p. 4, as cited in Rossi, *P.P.C.F.*, p. 139.

take reprisals. Was a dead German or an armload of grenades worth the lives of a dozen or more Frenchmen every time they struck?

Yes, said the Communists. "It was worth it. . . . Since repression affects all groups of society, it must eventually provoke a reaction which would permeate the entire population. It would push the nation as a whole to resist. Guerrilla fighting in a city means to attack constantly by every means, make every street a potential death trap for the occupier."[106] After a number of Frenchmen, mostly Communist, had been gunned down during a street demonstration by German soldiers, *L'Humanité* proclaimed:

> French blood has been spilled in the streets of Paris. Tomorrow all of France, responding to this summons from Paris, will rise in arms. . . . The resistance will become a tidal wave.[107]

Colonel Rémy, de Gaulle's personal envoy to military Resistance organizations in France, was the first of the General's agents to make contact with the F.T.P. Rémy reported in his Mémoires that he asked a Communist leader Joseph if it was necessary to kill German officers in order to get their arms. When Rémy questioned him about the resulting reprisals, Joseph replied: "At the news of the shooting of five or ten of our men we count fifty or one hundred enlistments in the F.T.P."[108]

So the F.T.P. kept up its terrorist activities, despite (if not because of) reprisals. The P.C.F. took great satisfaction in the fact that de Gaulle's 1941 cease-fire order came only twenty-four hours after an anti-terrorist statement by Vichyite Pétain:

---

106 Ehrlich, p. 58.
107 *L'Humanité*, August 21, 1941.
108 Rémy (pseud. for Renault Roulier), *Mémoirs d'un agent secret de la France libre* (Paris, 1948).

> We have laid down our arms. We do not have the right to take them up again to strike the Germans in the back.[109]

The Communists, of course, disagreed with Pétain and hinted that there was something wrong—like semi-collaborationist—with de Gaulle for not doing so. The non-Communist résistants, on the other hand, could well criticize the P.C.F., whose "Soviet first-France second" attitude had caused its about-face and subsequent "Johnny-come-lately" position.

The P.C.F. did pay the price, however, for its actions. Hundreds of hostages (some of them Communist leaders jailed by the Third Republic) were executed by the Nazis during the first year after the P.C.F. entered into active resistance against the Germans. Although the toll was great, the Party was well on its way to achieving the aim of making itself the post-war party of the Resistance, with the officials, heroes and martyrs (parti des fusillés) to substantiate the claim. The Communists wanted the final upsurge of the Resistance to be a mass uprising of an armed population and they wanted it to be controlled and directed by themselves. The Party thought that the price was worth the goal.

Their plans were excellent and well executed, but they did not succeed because they were blocked by one man: Charles de Gaulle.

---

109 Ehrlich, p. 58.

# Chapter V

# De Gaulle

General De Gaulle had been closely watching the Communists, since the Fall of France. Immediately following the capitulation on June 18, 1940, the General made his famous rallying cry for all Frenchmen to unite in a resistance to defeat the Nazi occupier. The Communists collaborated for another year and failed to heed at that time the call of de Gaulle, whom they labeled the "lackey of Anglo-Saxon capitalism."[110] The General paid little attention to this criticism as he set himself the task of strengthening the Free French in London and achieving recognition for them. De Gaulle did give much attention, however, to the P.C.F. when, in mid-1941, the party reversed itself to become an aggressive leader of the Resistance.

## SETTING

The Free French leader had mixed emotions about the entry of the Communists, not the Resistance. He feared their intentions but welcomed their assistance in a common effort. With more practicality than reconciliation, de Gaulle stated:

> There were no forces that should not be employed to beat the enemy, and I reckoned that theirs [the Communists'] had great weight in the kind of war imposed by the occupation.

---

110  De Gaulle, *War Mémoirs*, p. 267.

But de Gaulle added an important condition: "They would have to do so as part of a whole and, to be quite frank, under my control."[111] This condition was to prove to be a great source of conflict between the independent Communists, with their own political designs, and the sagacious de Gaulle, with his set of ideas and goals.

Having been ordered by Moscow to avoid all open conflict with de Gaulle's Free French Committee in London, the P.C.F. often found itself in a difficult position vis-à-vis de Gaulle, who claimed control over the whole Resistance movement inside France. The Party, however, resolved the dilemma between maintenance of their own independent forces or subordination of them to de Gaulle by building up the F.T.P. in deep secrecy. The Communists, while proclaiming a political solidarity with de Gaulle, concealed their military units even more from London than from the Germans, and the underground press only talked about them in the abstract. But de Gaulle was far from oblivious to what was going on. According to De Kerillis, "At the beginning of 1942 de Gaulle assured the British that the Communists were gaining ground in France and that there was a danger of a Russianized France after victory."[112]

## Unity of Action

For the sake of political expediency and for the common purpose of defeating the enemy, however, the P.C.F. did agree to a "unity of action" policy in mid-1942, after having been so advised by the Soviet Union. This alteration of line was nothing more than a superficial friendship with de Gaulle and other Resistance movements. Besides the fact that the "unity" policy made infiltration of other groups easier, the Communists needed more weapons and hoped that contact with London would help provide them.

---

111 *Ibid.*, p. 268.
112 Henri de Kerillis, *I Accuse de Gaulle* (New York, 1946).

Consequently, when de Gaulle's secret agent Rémy made his first contact with the Communists in France, he was told that the Communist groups needed arms, ammunition, and military specialists.[113] Such aid de Gaulle was reluctant to give. Nonetheless, this meeting, according to Jacques Soustelle, a top assistant to de Gaulle, resulted in the establishment of an information network between the Communists in France and the Free French in London and the "acceptance in principle" (but only that) by the Communists of a unified chief-of-staff for the occupied zone of France under the control of London.[114] The Secret Service of London would finance this organization, including the Communist forces involved. With approval from the Soviet Union, the P.C.F. agreed on November 15, 1942, to incorporate their paramilitary forces into the Forces of Fighting France (FFC).[115] A couple of months later, on January 14, 1943, Fernand Grenier, a member of the Central Committee of the P.C.F., arrived in London, bringing with him the formal adherence of the Communists to Fighting France for the duration of the war. He added, however, in a two-hour press conference that "the men who govern post-war France will be selected on the basis of what they have done to liberate the nation rather than on their political faith."[116] Grenier paid further lip service to de Gaulle by saying that all France was behind the General as the general champion of the liberation. But the friendship of the P.C.F. with General Henri Honoré Giraud indicated that the Communists thought he was the ideal man to lead the fighting forces in Africa. As the representative of the P.C.F., Grenier remained in London to protect his party's interests and serve as an information gatherer for the Central Committee.

---

113 Rémy, *Mémoirs*, p. 448.
114 Soustelle, *Envers et Contre Tout*, Vol. I, p. 390.
115 Rieber, pp. 26–7.
116 *New York Times*, January 15, 1943, p. 4.

In response to the "unity" policy, the P.C.F. began to coordinate efforts with other resistance réseaux. Reacting vigorously against the attempt of the Germans to deport French laborers, the Party helped to organize in co-operation with five other Resistance groups a massive strike of railroad workers in Lyon. In *L'Humanité*, the Party, while demanding greater efforts from its militants, urged non-Communist forces to swing into action. Said *L'Humanité* of December 4, 1942:

> Organize yourselves, form Corps Francs guerrilla units, and take to the hills, preparing yourselves for a guerilla war.[117]

### TWO OCCURRENCES

Two occurrences about this time influenced a much greater number of Frenchmen to heed this call than would have otherwise. One was the disbanding of the Vichy army by the Germans in November 1942 following the fall of North Africa and consequent occupation of the southern zone by the German army. There was some rumor that Giraud would come from North Africa to Vichy and march the French soldiers down to the Mediterranean, where they would meet an Allied invasion force. True or false, the Germans thought it best not to take chances. This freeing of thousands of men helped to fill the ranks of the guerrilla (or maquis) forces.

The other occurrence which served as a powerful influence for joining the maquis was the drafting of young Frenchmen to work in German factories, which began in early 1943. This forced labor drive gave the Frenchmen the easy choice of working against his country far away from home or for his country close to home. Many of these new recruits gave little thought to whom their organization was most directly linked—the P.C.F. or de Gaulle. They were fighting

---

117  *L'Humanité*, December 4, 1942.

first for France. However, Yves Farge, a Communist sympathizer who became the head to the important Comité d'action contre la Déportation (CAD), supplied money, false papers and, when possible, places of refuge for men fleeing the draft. As a result, many of these non-Communist refugees from enforced labor joined armed groups of resisters dominated and led by the Communists.

## Further Steps

Strengthened by the growing numbers of workers in the regular party resistance and the increasing number of maquis in the FTP, the P.C.F. took further steps to consolidate their power base, including a continuing friendship with de Gaulle, whose icon the Communists sported.

In an effort to extend their influence, the P.C.F. sought direct participation in the central bodies of the Gaullist overseas Resistance. This de Gaulle granted in an effort to give his government a more broadly democratic base. The offer came at a meeting of the Consultative Assembly at Algiers, which consisted of representatives of the Resistance, former deputies who had not voted to give full powers to Pétain, representatives of Overseas France, and other groups. Out of the total of 102 present, there were twenty-seven Communists, including André Marty and Fernand Grenier, P.C.F. representatives in Moscow and London respectively, and most of the former party deputies recently released from the Vichy prison in Algiers. There was much haggling over points of an acceptable resistance program and much agitation over representation in the important policy-making French Committee of National Liberation (CFLN), created on June 3, 1943, as an executive branch of the Fighting French movement. De Gaulle asked Grenier to participate. He replied that he would, provided certain proposals were accepted. Believing that submission to the Communist demands would be seen as weakness, de Gaulle refused. Recognizing the

P.C.F. as his most formidable rival for control of the Resistance, the General felt that if he granted the Communists too much they might ultimately try to force him to share his power with them. De Gaulle's refusal to grant a Communist the post of Commissar of Information came as a real disappointment to the Party, which recognized the propaganda value of the position. The party was somewhat appeased, however, when de Gaulle offered it the posts of Commissar of Air and Commissar of State, which were accepted, respectively, by Grenier and Francois Billoux.[118] Agreement on these positions was not reached, however, until April 1944, when the liberation of France was approaching. Rather than bicker about specifics, the Communists decided it was more important to have an established position in the provisional government when the Allies landed.

## Arms Dispute

De Gaulle was convinced that he was in a race with the Communists for post-war control of France. Thus, while he diplomatically tried to bring the Communists into a unified Resistance effort, giving them certain posts and granting certain requests for the sake of appeasement, he was exceedingly careful in his dealing with the Party.

Such was the case when de Gaulle gave orders in early 1943 to "Colonel Passy," André de Wavrin, the industrialist who controlled his arms-dropping organizations. The General told Passy that "no arms are to be parachuted directly to the Communists or dropped in such a way that they might fall into their hands."[119]

This negative response from de Gaulle was a real setback to the Communists, who as early as November 1942 had asked the

---

118  Rieber, pp. 55–8.
119  Passy, *Souvenirs: Missions Secrétes en France* (November 1942-June 1943), Paris, 1951, p. 164.

General for the "arms necessary to intensify the struggle against the German occupier." By August 1943, the P.C.F. was more desperate in its appeal: "The absence of sufficient arms is forcing us to limit our action against the Germans."[120] But de Gaulle, who normally would spare no effort to defeat the Germans, had serious reservations about how much aid to give the Communists. The P.C.F., however, decried bitterly in its clandestine press that: "In France we see the F.T.P., who alone are fighting, do not receive arms, whereas organizations which do nothing receive them. This is a scandal which must be ended."[121]

Emmanuel d'Astier de la Vigerie, the clever Commissar of the Interior in de Gaulle's government, was especially helpful to the Communists since his allegiance to the P.C.F. was unknown. D'Astier advocated sending more arms to the metropolitan resistance, largely under the control of the Communists, and he attacked the Bureau Central des Renseignements et d'Action (BCRA) for preventing arms shipments to France by their petty machinations. The BCRA, responsible for the transportation and distribution of agents and money to the internal Resistance, was accused by d'Astier of being particularly harmful to the Resistance.[122] At a meeting of the executive Action Committee of Fighting France, d'Astier supported a motion that would have subordinated the BCRA to General Giraud. According to Rieber, "the Communists believed it would be easier to obtain arms from Giraud than from the politically more astute de Gaulle."[123] The motion failed, for it was blocked by de Gaulle. Although this veto would indicate the General's astuteness, his failure to recognize d'Astier's true color might suggest the contrary.

---

120  Letters of the F.T.P. to General de Gaulle, dated November 23, 1942, and August 6, 1943, as cited in Rieber, p. 66.
121  *L'Humanité*, November 26, 1943.
122  Emmanuel d'Astier de la Vigerie, *Les Dieux et les hommes, 1943–1944* (Paris, 1952), p. 92.
123  Rieber, p. 67.

In any case, the behind-the-scenes efforts of the Communists for the purpose of obtaining arms are readily apparent.

## CORSICA

De Gaulle's fear of Communist tactics was strikingly reinforced by the liberation of Corsica in 1943. The Resistance in Corsica had been united in 1941 by a representative of de Gaulle, Major Colonna d'Istria. The FN, led by two Communists, Arthur Giovanni as political chief and Francois Vittorio as military chief, had agreed to serve under his command. In March 1943, d'Istria was captured and killed by the Italians. Soon afterward the FN committee, with a three to two Communist majority, entered into direct relations with Giraud, who had recently become the Commander-in-Chief of the Free French Army. Without discussing the situation in Corsica with de Gaulle, Giraud gave arms to the FN on his own initiative. De Gaulle later lamented that "Giraud did not breathe a word to me of the action he was taking in Corsica."[124] Meanwhile, the Communists were taking an additional step for the purpose of concentrating power in their hands. André Pourtalet, a former P.C.F. deputy who had been in contact with Giovanni for some time, went to Algiers to see Giraud. As a result of these maneuvers, the Communists controlled the distribution of arms sent by Giraud and also monopolized communications with Algiers. No other elements of the Resistance could reach Giraud, so they accepted the instructions of the FN. Thus, in Corsica the Communists, well-armed and in complete control of the Resistance, successfully demonstrated their technique for gaining power.

In his Mémoirs, de Gaulle displays his anger over the result of this technique, but he largely blames Giraud for the incident. De Gaulle recounts a later meeting with Giraud. Says de Gaulle:

---

124  De Gaulle, *Mémoirs*, p. 462.

"General, I am offended and disturbed by your manner
of proceeding in regard to me and the government by your
concealing your activities from us. I do not approve of the mo-
nopoly you have given to the Communist leaders. I consider it
unacceptable. . . ."[125]

De Gaulle's fears were further confirmed when, following the
surrender of Italy and the consequent occupation of Corsica by
troops from North Africa, the Communists exploited their strong
position to gain a large measure of political control through heavy
representation in local governments. To the Communists in Moscow
and France, however, the liberation of Corsica was a vindication of
their methods and a model for future action.

---

125 *Ibid.*, p. 464.

# Chapter VI

# Infiltration

The P.C.F. wanted the FN to be more than just "first" among the Resistance organizations. In order to keep the control and direction of the United Resistance effort in France, the Party wanted the FN to be the basis for the unification of all Resistance movements in France. Were this to happen, the Communists would have a much stronger bargaining position with de Gaulle in forming a post-war government. In order to accomplish this objective, the party began by infiltrating non-Communist organizations. This infiltration took place in all levels of the political and military resistance and in the trade union movement. By hard work and through the proper tactics, Communists eventually became elected representatives or appointed executives of a number of important committees and organizations.

## POLITICAL

As noted earlier,[126] the Communists had quite successfully penetrated Mouvements Unis de la Résistance (MUR), a large non-Communist mass political organization which was a fusion of three smaller groups in March 1943, and by 1944 the Communist influence in MUR had greatly increased. By infiltrating the MUR and other organizations, the P.C.F. managed to gain a strong position in the Conseil National de la Résistance (CNR). This body had been organized in 1943 by the legendary Jean Moulin, emissary of

---

126 *Supra*, p. 50.

de Gaulle. The CNR was supposed to coordinate the activities of the various resistance groups, political parties, and trade unions in France with those of the provisional government in Algiers. As the key link between France and Algiers, the CNR was a most important organization. When the Germans captured and shot Moulin at the end of 1943, there was an empty seat on the five-man permanent council. Already in control of two seats, the Communists won control of the third and from then on the policies of the CNR accurately reflected the desires of the Communists.[127] Because of its strong position in the CNR, the P.C.F. resisted all attempts to create a potential rival, especially one which was made up solely of Resistance groups and excluded political parties.

The only alternative to the CNR which the Communists would accept was incorporation of all Resistance groups into the FN. The Party received support for this idea from the Secretary-General of MUR, Pierre Hervé. Hervé, a loyal Communist, emphasized in his "Rapport Chardon" that the "National Front boldly carries on a policy of national union; it calls for initiative on the part of the masses; it strongly urges immediate action involving the broadest segments of population."[128] The only condition, however, for this "national union and immediate action" was that the leadership be Communist. According to Rieber, "Communist demands for unity meant complete acceptance of party leadership and doctrine."[129] This the non-Communists understandably would not accept.

## MILITARY

The P.C.F. employed similar tactics of infiltration in the military

---

127 Henri Michel, *Histoire de la Résistance* (Paris, 1950) pp. 49–51.
128 "Rapport Chardon," late 1943, as quoted in Henri Michel and B. Mirkine Guetzévitch, *Les Idées Politiques et Sociales de la Résistance* (Paris, 1954), p. 109.
129 Rieber, p. 91.

resistance and, with luck, managed to gain control of the most important military coordinating committee of the Resistance. The Comité d'Action Militaire (COMAC), one of the committees of the C.N.R., was established in the spring of 1944 for the purpose of uniting and directing the clandestine struggle. It was composed of three men, only one of whom was a Communist, Pierre Villon. However, by May 1944, a complex series of withdrawals and elections allowed a crypto-Communist to become a member. With two of its three members, the Party had gained control of COMAC.

As soon as this fact was established, de Gaulle created the Forces Francaises de l'Intérieur (FFI), to which he hoped to rally the various resistance groups. Without consulting the CNR, de Gaulle gave General Koenig the command of FFI. The Supreme Allied Headquarters recognized this command and by June 12th several American officers had been assigned to Koenig's chief of staff. Clashes inevitably broke out between COMAC and Koenig's command after the Allied invasion, when the Communists attempted to assert their influence over the FFI.

De Gaulle wanted to incorporate the various Resistance groups into the FFI with the National Committee in London as the command. The internal Resistance leaders rejected this, however, as they wished to keep their forces responsible to COMAC.[130] Thus, in May 1944, COMAC substantiated its claim to command the internal military Resistance and the Communists reinforced their control of COMAC. Later in the month another unexpected event further aided the Communists. Pontcarral, the chief of staff of COMAC and a non-Communist, was arrested by the Germans. A new election was held and, after some crafty maneuverings, a Communist, Alfred Malleret-Joinville, was elected as the new chief. Joinville, with the task of naming the chiefs of staff of most of the regional

---

130  *Ibid.*, pp. 96–7.

organizations, installed Communist appointees in Paris, Toulouse, Limoges, Marseilles, and Monpellier.[131]

Thus, on the eve of D-Day, the P.C.F., while calling for unity of action, maintained control of the national command of the military resistance. With its many regional and local commands, the party had extended its roots deep into the soil of the Resistance. Such a powerful base caused the non-Communists to question Communist intentions in the near future.

## TRADE UNIONS

While Communists infiltrated the political and military resistance, the Party increased its influence in the trade union movement. Says Rieber:

> As in their contacts with other Resistance groups, the Communists encouraged cooperation and unity of all trade-union elements on their terms in the common struggle against the enemy. They succeeded in reunifying the trade union movement in such a way that Communist influence in French labor organizations was greatly increased.[132]

This reunification followed the split which had taken place back in September 1939 following the Russo-German Pact. At that time the Communists had been officially ousted from the Confédération Général du Travail (C.G.T.), where they nonetheless had managed to maintain a significant following. After the German invasion of the U.S.S.R., the Party re-established contact with the non-Communist faction. There continued to be minor disputes between the two groups, but negotiations greatly improved the position of the P.C.F. The disruption of the organizational pattern

131 *Ibid.*
132 *Ibid.*, pp. 104–5.

of the C.G.T. caused by the war, occupation and German labor draft enabled the Communist labor cell, long experienced in underground organization, to exploit their newly won positions to great advantage. The strong Communist base in French labor not only aided the Party in its rivalry with other resistance organizations; it also enabled the P.C.F. to keep at a high level the factory sabotage and other activities disruptive to the Germans.

# Chapter VII

# Toward the Liberation

E ven though the Communists were in competition with other Resistance elements under the guise of unity, they left no doubt that the principal target of their efforts was the Nazi occupier, the hated "Boche." Control of the Resistance was important to the post-war planning of the P.C.F., but, more importantly, it enabled the Communists to use their own tactics for fighting Germans.

## SABOTAGE

These tactics included constant attack. Not one day of rest were the Germans allowed. Transportation facilities were hit the hardest as the FTP hammered away at trains, armored truck convoys, cars and bicycles.

Every night sabotage teams were on the prowl. One accomplishment was a train derailing which took the lives of 280 Germans. Another train mishap accounted for 180 victims.[133] In a London press conference, Fernand Grenier stated:

> "During the period from January to April 1943, 2000 railcars have been destroyed, and traffic has been interrupted at 17 places for more than 48 hours, each time on an important national line. In 31 places traffic has been stopped for 24 hours,

---

133 *Les Cahiers Francais*, "L'Armée Clandestine Francaise," (London, June 15, 1943), p. 9.

and in 75 cases for 12 hours. Two exploits were particularly remarkable. Two trains full of German troops heading for the East were derailed. When the Germans attempted to escape they were killed by grenade or machine gun. Not one escaped. In one operation we had no losses. In the other, we had seven wounded or killed."[134]

The Germans were plagued as well by continuing industrial sabotage which extended from tank factories to places where food was prepared for Nazi armies. Reports of these sabotage attempts were given in many newspapers. For example, the *New York Times* said: "Many Germans on the Russian front have died because of preserves made in the French factories."[135] As D-Day approached, all sabotage efforts accelerated. The leaders of this sabotage—train, tank, food, and otherwise—continued to be the Communists.

## CLANDESTINE PRESS

Ever aware of the value of propaganda, the P.C.F. maintained a large and vociferous clandestine press which had proven itself an influential element of the Resistance. The widespread Communist activities against the Boche and the progress of the Party in the different aspects of the Resistance would have been less significant, had the Communist press left Frenchmen unaware of their gains. This *L'Humanité* and other Communist or sympathizing papers would not allow.

*L'Humanité* published 317 numbers during the occupation, and such regional clandestine issues as La Marseillaise in Marseilles and Le Patriote in Lyon kept their areas well aware of Communist successes. Despite severe repressive measures, by mid-1944 the Communists controlled thirty-one daily papers, which were authorized

---

134 *Ibid.*
135 *New York Times,* Jan 15, 1943, p. 4.

to publish over 20,000 copies each and issued in all 2,815,000 copies, or 26.8 percent of the French press.[136] Many of the readers during the Resistance were not Communists. Appealing for a "unity of action," the Communist press called upon these people to join one of the front organizations. Identifying the Communists as a group of patriots committed only to the liberation of France and the establishment of democracy, the party literature made no mention of the party's plan to gain control of the government.

## MAQUIS

The maquis, or guerrilla fighters, continued to make a most important contribution to the total Resistance effort. The Communist maquis were the Francs Tireurs et Partisans who, time and again, demonstrated their finesse in guerrilla warfare techniques. In addition to the sabotaging of trains, the F.T.P. by 1944 were performing numerous ambushes of German detachments. During the first two years of active Resistance, ambushes were few in number, as risks were great and guns were few. The maquis, F.T.P. or otherwise, were also few in number until 1943. At this time, two events, the German forced-labor drive and the disbanding of the Vichy army, caused the ranks of the maquis to swell.[137]

As the maquis forces grew larger and gained more arms and experience, they expanded the range and variety of their activities. Although maquis units were scattered all over France, their ideal ground was rough terrain, especially in the thinly populated areas where occupation troops were not as concentrated. In the northern zone, such places were Brittany, the mountains of the Jura and the Vosges. In the south there were many areas well-adapted for guerrilla activity, including the whole Massif Central.[138] In all of these areas

---

136 Jean Mottin, *Histoire Politique de la Presse, 1944–49* (Paris, 1949), p. 31.
137 *Supra*, pp. 60–61.
138 Ehrlich, *Résistance*, p. 142.

the F.T.P. led the maquis activity, be it sabotage, ambush, or snip-
ing. The countryside was not the only domain, however, of maquis
activity as cities often were prey. In La Rochelle and Rochefort the
maquis maintained a virtually continuous sabotage of railway sheds
and telephone and electric lines. German army trucks were wrecked
with mortars and supply depots were set on fire.[139] In Paris, Germans
returning for "rest" from Russia and Yugoslavia were grenaded in
the Rex theater.[140] This increasing pressure on the Germans came
as a result of accelerated maquis activity. As D-Day approached,
the Francs-Tireurs et Partisans, already a third of the total maquis
forces, increased not only its numerical strength but also the pace
of its activity. As German defeat seemed increasingly inevitable,
many former "attentistes" became opportunists or glory-seekers by
joining the Resistance. In doing so, they nonetheless contributed
momentum to the movement, and especially to the maquis units.
Needless to say, the Communists attracted their share of newcomers
and used them to good advantage.

## "Post-D-Day"

After the Normandy invasion on D-Day, June 6, 1944, the
principal purpose of the approximately 70,000[141] Francs-Tireurs
et Partisans was to seek out and destroy the enemy. They were also
to cooperate with the Allied forces. The F.T.P. directed their efforts
toward the liberation of territory lying behind the German lines,
the disruption of German communications and transportation,
and the replacement of the Vichy administration. They also tried to
arouse and organize the population in order to harass the Germans
in their retreat and assist the Allies in their advance.[142]

---

139 *New York Times*, March 10, 1943, p. 7.
140 *Ibid.*, January 15, 1943, p. 4.
141 This figure was given in de Gaulle, *Mémoirs*, pp. 588, 590.
142 Rieber, p. 126.

At the same time, the Communist propaganda machine was doing its work. Party militants and front organizations were urged to fight with all means at their disposal. The F.T.P. was encouraged to attack both the German troops and the hated Vichy militia. Leaflets, newspapers, and wall inscriptions everywhere proclaimed: "Unite! Arm! Fight!"[143]

During the four months of the Liberation, from D-Day to the end of September 1944, the P.C.F. cooperated with other Resistance elements, but it continued to lead and bear the major part of the effort. Everywhere Communist cells were at work. The F.T.P. greatly stepped up its efforts and Communist-run COMAC coordinated most of the military resistance. With Communist Joinville as the head of the underground army in France and Communists in charge of Paris and other key regions, the "behind-the-scenes" fighting against the Nazis was indeed in the hands of the Communists. Though the first goal of the P.C.F. was to rid France of the Germans and, in so doing, aid the Soviet Union, the Communists never lost sight of their other goal—post-war power. The Communists knew their chances of obtaining the second goal were directly related to how successful they were in obtaining the first. De Gaulle was glad to receive assistance from the Communists for the first goal; however, he was all too worried about the second.

Whatever the priority of its goals, the P.C.F. threw itself with tremendous force into the task of ridding France of Germans. The Communists tried to infuse the population with the traditional spirit of revolution. The Party wanted a "levée en masse [uprising] for revenge, for liberty, and for the independence and greatness of our country."[144] The P.C.F. prompted the formation of patriotic militias of armed minutemen in every city block, section, factory and town. These militias, which included many former "non-resisters," were

---

143 *Ibid.*, p. 127.
144 *L'Avant-Garde*, June 15, 1944, as quoted in Rieber, p. 128.

to play a leading role in the liberation of French territory behind German lines.

With encouragement and directives coming from the self-exiled leader, Maurice Thorez, the P.C.F. set itself diligently to directing an armed insurrection against the Boche. The F.T.P. was everywhere. With its greatly increased number of men, the F.T.P. could afford to have groups of several thousand men in many different areas of the country.

The F.T.P. continued to demonstrate a rare courage and inspiration. A non-Communist commander of the FFI in Brittany, Colonel Eon, declared: "I always found the FTP inspired by a will to fight and a hatred of the Germans which surpassed that of any other unit formed by any other organization."[145] According to Monsieur and Madame Roger Pansart, non-Communist Resistance leaders in the St. Malo area: "The Communists were willing to take chances that no one else would take. This was especially true after the Normandy invasion. . . ."[146]

## PARIS

The liberation of Paris put the Communists in an excellent position to demonstrate their metal and strengthen their bid for post-war power. The head of the underground army in Paris was a Communist, as were many other top leaders. The party dominated the unions and the clandestine press. It ran two of Paris' three Resistance political committees and had turned the third into an ineffective debating society. For months the Communists had been reinforcing their positions, and planting their agents in key posts in every part of the city. Even a senior Resistance doctor complained that the party had forced a watchful deputy on him.[147]

---

145 Robert Aron, *Histoire de la Libération de la France* (Paris, 1945), p. 112.
146 Interview with M. and Mme. Roger Pansart, July 6, 1967.
147 Larry Collins and Dominique Lapierre, *Is Paris Burning?* (New York,

De Gaulle was afraid the Communist control of the underground in Paris would give the Party an eventual springboard to power. He believed the P.C.F. intended to launch a bloody insurrection that would result in Communist possession of the levers of power. By the time he and his government entered Paris, de Gaulle's reasoning ran, the Communists would have implanted themselves in the governing structures of France. They would have confronted him with an entrenched Red-run Commune.[148]

The Communists were indeed advocates of insurrection in Paris. However, this question of how best to liberate the capital was a source of sharp disagreement between COMAC and the supreme command of the FFI in London. COMAC, supported by the P.C.F., by the Paris Committee of Liberation, and by other elements of the CNR, wanted to turn Paris into a battlefield by trying to block a German withdrawal through the city. They anticipated street fighting, the building of barricades, and the liberation of Paris by Parisians before the Allies arrived. On the other hand, General de Gaulle and other more moderate elements of the Resistance wanted to harass the enemy without provoking him into a house-by-house defense that could well destroy the city.

The Communists came to accept the value of a temporary "unity of action" policy with other Resistance forces and the government of General de Gaulle. The political risks were too great for the Communists to pursue doggedly their own unilateral policies. If a Communist uprising were crushed, then an anti-Communist regime might well be built on the ruins of Paris. Another consideration was the comparative disadvantage in arms which the Communists had in relation to the Nazis. Furthermore, a Communist attempt to seize power would have failed because

---

1965), pp. 26–7.
148 *Ibid.*, p. 24.

of the preponderance of Anglo-American arms.[149]

With these considerations in mind, the Communist-led insurrection did not take place, despite high tension in Paris and P.C.F. desires to the contrary. Opposition in Paris was expressed through continued sabotage, sniper deaths, and distribution of the clandestine press. As the Allied forces drew nearer and defeat was on the doorstep, the Nazi commander of Paris, General von Cholitz, disobeyed Hitler's orders to blow up the city[150] and surrendered on August 25, 1944.

### AFTERMATH

The Allied momentum continued, and, by the end of September 1944 most of France had been cleared of German troops. The heroic period of the Resistance was over and the most heroic of Resistance groups, the French Communist Party, was faced with making the difficult transition from a clandestine fighting force to a legal mass party. The P.C.F. did not gain control of the post-war government but, thanks to its wartime accomplishments, it gained a very respectable position in the eyes of the people as the "party of the Resistance." The P.C.F. was the party of heroes and fusillés. As such, the Party enjoyed a large voice in the affairs of the post-war provisional government and in the establishment of a permanent government.

---

149  Rieber, p. 154.
150  Collins and Lapierre, *passim.*

# Conclusion

In the five-year period from the outbreak of the war to the liberation, the P.C.F. had completed an amazing metamorphosis. Denounced as traitors to France during the first two years of the war, the Communists had emerged from the war as "the most heroic of patriots." The early vacillation of the party and the "Johnny-come-lately" tag were all but forgotten by most Frenchmen, in light of the tremendous contribution the P.C.F. made to the defeat of the enemy. Instead, the resolve, the courage, and the determination of the last three years were remembered. Consequently, the P.C.F. was much stronger than it had ever been before. In so much as it was, the Party had indeed accomplished the objective of establishing itself in a position of post-war power. Takeover was no longer the order of the day, at least by violent means. The Party, however, with its newly-won strength, realized that control of the government might eventually be obtained through legal channels.

That this was realized is significant. It meant that the P.C.F. had been brought a little closer to the mainstream of French political life, even though it was still on the far left. Many French Communists who once had militantly placed the Soviet Union way above their native land had become so involved in the unified patriotic struggle that they had indeed become patriots again.

In its performance over the period from August 1939 to August 1944, the P.C.F. had proven several things about itself. First of all, it demonstrated that it was a party of great vitality. The party might waver in its stand as situations changed, but once a stand was taken, the party wholeheartedly defended that stand. Thus, in the first stage, no party on the French political scene was more adamant in its opposition to the Nazis. In fact, no political group was so outspoken concerning any subject. Thus, in the second stage, the P.C.F. demonstrated, once the decision was made, how devastating its opposition to the French war effort could be. When the Germans first occupied France, they were in relative peace and security, despite de Gaulle's trumpet call to resist. Yet, one year later, when the "semi-legal" collaborators reversed their stand with the Nazi attack of the U.S.S.R., the Germans quickly learned what a difference it could make to have the Communists as their enemies. Well-experienced in the clandestine techniques, the P.C.F. charged the Resistance with a life and energy that no other group could have given so well. The Party's vitality was constantly in search of an outlet and found several in its increasingly severe attacks against the Nazis, its infiltration of other resistance groups and, finally, its control of the Resistance. The great contribution made by the P.C.F. in the Liberation was a crowning testimony to the Party's zeal and energy.

The P.C.F. also demonstrated a high degree of organization matched by no other political party or Resistance group. This organization had been nurtured in the period before the war, but it was greatly developed during the war. Excellent training, unquestioned adherence to regulations, and vertical organization were all keys to the Communist success in the Resistance movement.

The vitality and organization of the party were largely due to a third quality which the Communists possessed, namely purpose. What more noble purpose could one have that to elevate the welfare and dignity of the repressed lower classes? Many French workers were originally attracted by such a purpose. The Soviet Union seemed to them to be a bright light in a dark world because of this purpose. Such a purpose inspired militancy and commanded devotion. Vitality and organization were only natural by-products. The ideology of "Russia first, France second" followed, as loyalty was spontaneous to this Champion of the Lower Classes. The sacrifices which the P.C.F. made during the war and the repression it received were bearable because of this high purpose.

With this vitality, organization, and purpose, it is no wonder that the French Communists had such a tremendous influence on the Resistance movement against the Nazis. It is no wonder that they were able to infiltrate so many other groups while attracting large numbers of non-Communists into their National Front. It is no wonder that de Gaulle so greatly feared their intentions, while welcoming their assistance. Nor is it surprising that the Communists controlled both the political resistance and the military resistance in France for the last year of German occupation.

The P.C.F. had paid a great price. To say the least, despite its self-serving motives, it richly deserved the acclaim, status, and power it enjoyed in post-war France.

# Bibliography

In researching any subject dealing with the Communist Party, one begins with the difficulty posed by the very secretive nature of its operations. An axiomatic practice of most Communist parties, especially of those within a non-Communist state, is to pay strict adherence to numerous regulations protecting their security. Such has been the case of the French Communist Party throughout the history of its existence. However, under the special clandestine conditions to which all resistance organizations were subject in opposing the Nazi activities, the Communists had to pay even greater attention to a multitude of rules set down by the party leadership for guarding the safety of the Party and its members. Making the slightest mistake could lead to arrest, imprisonment, and execution. Even worse, it could give information to the Nazi authorities which would lead to the detection and consequent jeopardy of other Communist members. Thus, maximum security was necessary and it was maintained by the well-disciplined P.C.F. in its resistance to the Germans.

Such conditions were understandably not conducive to the maintenance of records or documents. In fact, most papers were destroyed after having served their temporary purpose. Another precaution exercised by the Communists, especially when transporting a written message from one place to another, was to put the message into a special code. Numerous other precautions were heeded. The net effect has been to leave a dearth of valuable primary source material to those who could research the role of the Communist Party in the French resistance movement. The greatest authority on the subject of the French Resistance movement, Henri Michel, has given even another reason for this lack of available documents concerning French Communist activity. He states: "The documents published after the war are relatively rare. The party has chosen, in presenting them skillfully, those which would facilitate its propaganda."[151] Michel also mentions the problem confronting those searching for such primary source material as memoirs. He says: "In the abundant literature which expresses the memoires of Resistance workers, there is very little from Communists. . . . The real reason for this is the regulation which forbids members of the party to express a personal point of view."[152]

Interviews and correspondence with Communist participants in the Resistance should be helpful, but here again there are several problems. Many of the most active Communist "résistants" did not survive the second World War, and of those who did many are not alive today. With the few who are living today one must exercise caution as the tendency to exaggerate, whether from faulty memories or intentionally, is almost universal.

*L'Humanité* and other smaller Communist publications produced clandestine issues during the Resistance despite the constant threat of severe penalty for doing so. These newspapers and journals are good primary sources for reflecting the official party stance toward certain issues. They also served to advise and encourage party members. Yet the clandestine press was not only quite biased, as would be expected, but it also can only portray to a limited degree the total role of the Communists in the Resistance effort.

Contemporary histories and memoires are fairly good primary sources. Among the best memoires available are those of Maurice

151 Henri Michel, *Bibliographie critique de la Résistance* (Paris, 1964), p. 90.
152 *Ibid.*

Thorez, Emmanuel d'Astier de la Vigerie, and Charles de Gaulle.

Surprisingly the war-time issues of the *New York Times* give a fair amount of factual information concerning the Communists' participation in the Resistance. Heed must be paid in assessing the credibility of news reported by the *Times*, but even so some valuable background information can be obtained.

There are several secondary sources which are quite helpful. The most valuable of secondary sources are Rossi's books, which contain much original material, including reproduction of tracts, pamphlets and letters. Rossi is more helpful for the first two periods, whereas Rieber is of great assistance in understanding the third period. These and other secondary sources are listed in later pages.

All in all, however, he who would undertake to research comprehensively the role of the Communists in the French Resistance must accept this lack of adequate and objective primary source material. Using what materials he has, though limited, subjective and biased they be, the author has attempted to piece together a number of scattered parts into an accurate and acceptable reconstruction of the role of the P.C.F. in the Resistance movement.

# I. PRIMARY SOURCES

## A. Personal

### 1. Interviews

Michel, Henri. Paris, June 29, 1967.

Pansart, M. et Mms. Roger. St. Malo, July 6, 1965.

> These were more helpful for general than for specific knowledge. They are further discussed in the acknowledgments.

## 2. Letter

Lecoeur, Auguste. To the author, January 18, 1968. This was helpful for an understanding of certain major points.

## 3. Collected Writings

Thorez, Maurice, *Oeuvres de Maurice Thorez*, Vol. XIX, Bk. IV (Paris, 1958); Bk. V (Paris, 1959).

_____, *Pour L'Union, Le Front Francais* (Paris, 1947).

Thorez's writings are indispensable for official party opinion and are reflections of party propaganda.

## 4. Memoirs

D'Astier, Emmanuel de la Vigerie, *Sept Jours en Exil* (Paris, 1946).

_____, *Sept Fois Sept Jours* (Paris, 1947).

_____, *Les Dieux et Les Hommes* (Paris, 1952).

Since crypto-Communist d'Astier was the leader of the Movement *Libération*, his books are helpful for understanding P.C.F. infiltration techniques. He describes his relation with de Gaulle.

Benouville, Guillian de, *Unknown Warrior* (New York, 1949). A prejudicial but interesting account of the life and atmosphere involved in clandestine fighting.

Blum, Léon, *L'Histoire Jugera* (Montreal, 1943). Blum discussed his relationship with Communists during the early part of the war; reflects socialist opinion.

De Wavrin, André [Passy], *Missions Sécretes en France*, November 1942-June 1943 (Paris, 1951).

_____, *Deuxiéme Bureau Londres* (Monte Carlo, 1947).

_____, *10, Duke Street, Londres* (Monte Carlo, 1948).

These three books comprise the memoirs of Colonel Passy, the military director of the B.C.R.A. They are fascinating reading and valuable, both for background and specifics.

De Gaulle, Charles, *The War Memoirs of Charles de Gaulle* (New York, 1964). De Gaulle's *Memoirs* are essential to the thesis for the discussion of Communist-Gaullist relations and for other facts.

Renault-Roulier, Gilbert [Rémy], *Memoirs d'un Agent Secret de la France*

*Libre* (Paris, 1946). Deals with the relations between Free France and the internal Resistance movement, including the Communists.

Soustelle, Jacques, *Envers et Contre Tout*. 2 vols. Paris, 1947 and 1950. Another personal account of relationships between the Free French and internal Resistance movements. Volume 2 gives a good description of Communist infiltration methods.

As noted earlier, Memoirs and Reminescences of Communist resistance workers were forbidden. Thus, they are rare. This is most unfortunate for those who would research the Communist resistance activities.

## B. Contemporary newspapers

*L'Humanité* (Paris), August 1939-August 1944. Valuable as mouthpiece of party opinion and as source of propaganda.

*New York Times*, 1940–1944. Gives helpful, factual information.

## C. Contemporary tracts, pamphlets, letter

"Daladier-Chamberlain-Mussolini-Franco & Pie XII," a tract, March 1940.

Thorez, Maurice and Duclos, Jacques, a letter addressed in the name of the Central Committee, February 1940.

"Le Peuple pend les traities," a pamphlet, Fall 1941.

Since all of the above issues were illegal, they were not officially published. All, however, were distributed in Paris and some in other places. The first four sources above are reproduced in A. Rossi's *Les Communistes Francais Pendant la Drôle de Guerre*; the last one was reproduced in Rossi's *La Guerre des Papillons*. These sources and other valuable pamphlets, tracts, and letters reproduced in Rossi but not quoted in the thesis are of utmost importance for understanding the position of the P.C.F.

## D. Contemporary magazines

*Les Cahiers Francais*, London, June 1943-April 1944.

*Inside France*, French News Service, New York, May 25, 1940-June 15, 1940.

These magazines had material of specific importance to the thesis; in addition, there were several good articles for background.

### E. Contemporary histories

Marty, André, *The Trial of the French Communist Deputies*, London, 1941.
This book discusses what happened in the trial of the French Communist deputies in Paris in March-April 1940.

# II. SECONDARY SOURCES

### A. General Histories

Aron, Robert, *Histoire de la Libération*. Paris, 1955. A factual understanding of the liberation.

Atkinson, Littleton B., *Communist Influence on French Rearmament*. Maxwell A.F. Base, Ala., 1955. Good for one quote, but otherwise irrelevant.

Borkenau, Franz, *European Communism*. London, 1953. Most helpful in understanding the role of the P.C.F. and some of the problems facing it.

Caute, David, *Communism and the French Intellectuals*. New York, 1964. Contributes largely to understanding of French intellectuals during the Resistance.

Cogniot, George, *Les Intellectuals et la Renaissance Francaise*. Paris, 1945. Supplementary to Caute.

Collins, Larry and Lapierre, Dominique, *Is Paris Burning?* New York, 1965. Gives a very interesting and descriptive account of the Liberation of Paris and events leading up to it, including pressure on the Nazi general to burn the city.

De Kerillis, Henry, *I Accuse de Gaulle*. New York, 1946. Though marred by extreme partisanship, it has some interesting material about Communist attitude to Giraud and de Gaulle.

Ehrlich, Blake, *Resistance: France, 1940–45*. New York, 1965. An overly dramatic but helpful account of the French Resistance movement.

Fauvet, Jacques, *Histoire du Parti Communiste Francais*. Vol.2. Paris, 1964. Has good but superficial discussion of Communists in the Resistance; leaves many gaps.

Lecoeur, August, *Le Partisan*. France, 1963. A short, personal history that adds to thesis.

Lorwin, Val R., *The French Labor Movement*. Cambridge, Mass., 1954. Discussion of relationship between P.C.F. and C.G.T.

Micaud, Charles, *Communism and the French Left*. U.S.A., 1963. Helpful for background.

Michel, Henri, *Histoire de la Résistance (1940–1944)*. Paris, 1950. A short precise history.

_____, *Les Courants de Pensée de la Résistance*. Paris, 1962.

_____, and Guetzévitch, B.M., *Les Idées Sociales et Politiques de la Résistance*. Paris, 1954.

These two books are excellent discussions of Resistance thought.

Mottin, Jean, *Histoire Politique de la Presse*. Paris, 1949. Helpful information on Communist propaganda.

Osgood, Samuel M., *The Fall of France*. U.S.A., 1965. Several essays on why France fell so quickly to the Germans.

Palmer, R.R., *History of the Modern World*. New York, 1964.

Rieber, Alfred J., *Stalin and the French Communist Party*. New York, 1962. An excellent work which adds considerably to understanding Communist activity in the Resistance.

Rossi, A. [Tasca, Angelo], *Les Communistes Francais Pendant la Drôle de Guerre*. Paris, 1951.

_____, Physiologie du Parti Communiste Francais. Paris, 1948.

_____, La Guerre des Papillons. Paris, 1954.

All three of these books are well-researched and were invaluable to the author.

Tillion, Charles, *Les F.T.P.* France, 1962. Contains many detailed stories of the F.T.P. activities by its Commander-in Chief.